MARTHA STEWART'S
VERY
GOOD
THINGS

For information about permission to reproduce selections from this book, write to trade.permissions@hmhco.com or to Permissions, Houghton Mifflin Harcourt Publishing Company, 3 Park Avenue, 19th Floor, New York, New York 10016.

www.hmhbooks.com
www.marthastewart.com

Library of Congress Cataloging-in-Publication Data is available.

ISBN: 978-1-328-50826-3

ISBN: 978-1-328-50670-2 (ebook)

Printed in China

MM 10 9 8 7 6 5 4 3 2 1

MARTHA STEWART'S
VERY GOOD THINGS

Clever Tips & Genius
Ideas for an Easier,
More Enjoyable Life

From the editors
of Martha Stewart

Houghton Mifflin Harcourt
Boston New York 2021

PRODUCED BY MELCHER MEDIA

Contents

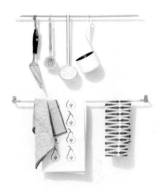

Introduction

I clearly recall when "It's a good thing" became my personal catchphrase, back in the early nineties. I had just painted the handles of my gardening hand tools a bright orange, so they could not possibly be lost in the chaos of the garden, and the phrase just came to me. At the time, it immediately struck a chord with the director and producers of my TV show, and of course shortly thereafter with our viewers. I continued to use it on a very regular basis to call out solutions and projects that were simple, smart, and sensible.

Since then, Good Things has been an unwaveringly important—and an in-demand—part of *Martha Stewart Living*, always presented in the beginning of the magazine. Indeed, these ideas are what readers turn to first and use with avid regularity in their own homes and lives.

What qualifies as a Good Thing? The idea must be straightforward but yield a surprising result—for example, decanting liquid dish soap from unattractive plastic dispensers into decorative glass bottles fitted with excellent pourers that look beautiful and perform well on every sink top (see page 53). Or, conversely, it could be an unexpected means to achieve a desired end, such as employing ice cubes to smooth iron-free sheets (page 61). It should call for easy-to-find materials, often used in novel ways—like enlisting a garden lattice as an organizer (page 100). And sometimes it's about repurposing what you already have, such as mismatched bowls that double as jewelry holders (page 97). It should absolutely be useful and relevant—and, of course, beautiful.

Curated in this single volume is the best of the best, from 30 years of Good Things, presented in practical chapters: Decorating, Homekeeping (which covers gardening), Organizing, Cooking, Entertaining, and Celebrating. We even pay homage to "classic" Good Things, like the indispensable stain chart from 2004 (page 62), and our best practices, like labeling serving dishes before hosting a big dinner to identify where food will go (page 171).

Old or new, the clever ideas here are all designed to make your life easier and more enjoyable—and that's always a good thing!

Martha Stewart

Open-Shelf
Backdrop,
PAGE 22

1

Decorating

Beauty is in the details. Elevate your home with some simple tricks and techniques—an eye-catching pop of color on a window frame, for example, or a custom headboard made with patterned textiles. There are plenty of such notions in this chapter, along with simple yet surprising DIY projects for creating one-of-a-kind furniture, lighting, and accent pieces using the most ordinary of supplies. Plus, you'll find design-pro painting secrets that bring serious style.

Furniture

Custom Cabinet Pulls

Looking to add a hit of luxe to a wardrobe (or buffet or bar cabinet)? Wrap the handles in leather tape, designed to patch rips and tears in furniture and other leather goods. The handsome adhesive, sold online, will provide extra cushion for your hands too. At the top of each handle, wrap a length of tape once around and secure at the back with a few stitches, using an upholstery needle and heavy-duty cotton thread. Continue wrapping down the pull in a spiral, overlapping about ½ inch. Fold tape to be flush with the bottom of the pull, then trim excess and stitch to secure.

WEEKEND PROJECT

Linen-Front Cabinet ⟩

Line glass doors with gauzy linen, and a storage unit is instantly more stylish—and practical, since the contents on the inner shelves will not be as visible. The best part? The easy project calls for adhesives and no hemming or hammering—meaning you can swap out the fabric on a whim.

TOOLS & MATERIALS

Cabinet with glass doors

Measuring tape

Open-weave linen fabric

Scissors

Double-sided tape dots

Gaffers' tape

1. Carefully remove glass from doors. Measure panes; trim fabric to at least 1 inch larger on all sides, following horizontal lines of fabric's warp.

2. Put double-sided tape dots at corners; attach on inside frame. Cover edges with gaffers' tape.

 Tip — For even more camouflaging, use fabric with more opacity, such as cotton, and in a striking print or more subdued solid.

Modern Desk

A bespoke desk is a great way to personalize your work space. Mix-and-match tabletops and legs, found online, make creating one easy—and are easy on the budget. Some tables have pre-drilled holes, or you'll need to do this yourself—such as when adding midcentury-style hairpins like these.

TOOLS & MATERIALS
Construction adhesive, such as Liquid Nails

Plywood, ½ inch thick (cut to match table dimensions)

Putty knife

Stainless steel table (this one is 47¼-by-23⅝-inches)

Sandpaper, 100 grit

4 powder-coated hairpin legs and screws

Pencil

Drill with ⅛-inch bit

1. Squeeze adhesive onto plywood; spread with putty knife. Place table on top of plywood, aligning edges; weigh with stacks of books at either end. Let dry overnight.

2. With sandpaper, smooth edges and clean up any drips of adhesive. Flip tabletop so it's plywood-side up. Position a leg 1 inch from corner. Use a pencil to mark screw-hole locations. Repeat for all corners.

3. Drill pilot holes into tabletop at pencil marks. Reposition leg and screw it in. Repeat for all legs.

Bedside Shelf

No room for a nightstand? A floating shelf-and-bracket combo provides a roomy enough place for all the niceties without taking up precious floor space. And a Carrara or other marble tile from a home improvement store is a posh alternative to standard (read: engineered wood) shelves, to beautify your bedroom. Here the sleek slab is paired with sturdy walnut shelf brackets, for warmth (metal supports could read as cold, not cozy). You can swap these out with other types of wood, depending on your design scheme (note how the walnut complements the rattan headboard). Mount the brackets evenly apart, 2 or 3 inches from either end; the shelf should be just above mattress height and about 6 inches from the edge of the bed. Rest the tile on top, adhering it to the brackets with epoxy glue for extra security. Curate the items here for calm, not clutter.

Paint

Strong Focal Point

Painting the trim of a fireplace a dramatic cobalt blue (or your own must-have hue) can bring a whole new energy to a room. Start with a primer tinted the same shade, and you'll achieve a saturated finish with fewer coats of paint. Double the impact with artwork that echoes the bold color.

Tips

PLAN AHEAD
Before you begin any painting project, line roller trays with plastic wrap. That way you can just peel it off—no rinsing required.

PROTECT YOUR PHONE
Seal your cell in a zip-top plastic bag so you can talk or text without covering it in paint.

KEEP THE SAME TOOLS
Instead of having to clean them during a paint project, cover brush bristles and rollers in plastic wrap and freeze the tools in a resealable bag; they'll thaw in 15 to 30 minutes.

Window Detailing

Inject a small dose of vibrant color into an otherwise neutral scheme by painting just the inner mullions of a window. High-gloss paint works best. Bonus: This sunny yellow will brighten your space (and spirits) on even dark and dreary days.

Decorative Edge

Sometimes all it takes is a sliver of paint to punch up a space, like with this red-rimmed desk (the edges of a table or bookshelf would work too). Use a brush or roller that's about the same width so you can cover the strip in one smooth stroke. More style points: Spray-paint a task lamp's dome to match.

Tip

To ensure sharp lines, put painters' tape around the desktop's perimeter. Then rub it firmly with a credit card for a tight seal.

High-Gloss Makeover

With just a couple of coats of glossy black (or white, if you prefer) spray paint, any estate-sale find can go from frumpy to fabulous. Work on a drop cloth in a well-ventilated area.

TOOLS & MATERIALS

Sturdy vintage table
Screwdriver and/or painters' tape
Rotary sanding tool and sandpaper, 150 grit
Tack cloth
Primer and lacquer spray paint

1. Remove hardware with a screwdriver, or protect it with painters' tape.

2. Sand table, using a rotary tool on the legs; wipe with a tack cloth. Coat with primer and let dry; sand and wipe again.

3. Coat with lacquer spray paint. Let dry, then lightly sand and wipe it down. Finish with a second coat.

Patterned Folding Stools

Portable camp stools are as functional (and stylish!) indoors as they are on a beach. Enlist them in an entryway or guest room, or whenever/wherever you need temporary seating. Buy stools with plain canvas fabric and give them custom colors: Detach each seat from its base and lay it on a drop cloth. Create patterns with painters' tape or geometric stencils (or go freestyle); apply craft paint with a brush or foam applicator. Let dry overnight, then remove tape and stencils and reassemble stool.

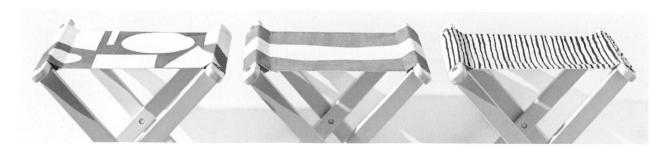

Rubber Band Trick

For drip-free painting, use this tip that appeared in the February 2004 issue of *Martha Stewart Living*: Stretch a large rubber band over the open can. This way you can gently wipe the tip of the brush against the band (not the can's rim) each time you dip it.

Embellished Dresser Drawers

Here's a whimsical way to give an already handsome piece an added layer of charm: Paint the sides of the drawers for a special treat every time you open them. Practically any palette will do, but this silvery blue-green combination (the trim is painted in a lighter shade) contrasts nicely with the warmth of the wood. More updates: Line the drawers in a color-coordinated self-adhesive wallpaper or shelf liner, and swap out the knobs (these have brass details that echo the tray on top).

Tip

For the two-tone effect on the drawer sides, first tape off what will be the darker section; apply two coats of paint with a 3-inch angled brush, letting it dry each time. Then tape around the strip at the bottom; apply two coats of lighter paint with a 1-inch angled brush.

Eye-Catching Cabinet

To revive a tired antique—like this barrister bookcase, with its glass fronts—paint it inside and out. Don't skip the prep: Proper sanding is the secret to a polished result, both before you begin and also between coats.

TOOLS & MATERIALS

Cabinet

Screwdriver

Sandpaper, 150 grit and 220 grit

Tack cloth

Primer and paint

Flat brush, mini roller, and angled brush

1. Remove hardware with screwdriver. Sand all over with 150-grit sandpaper, then wipe it down with a tack cloth.

2. Apply a coat of primer with a flat brush; let dry.

3. Apply paint color with mini roller; use angled brush for hard-to-reach spots and details. Let dry.

4. Apply two to three more coats, rubbing with 220-grit sandpaper and wiping down after each coat dries.

WAYS TO

PAINT WOOD FLOORS

Putting paint on a wood floor will imbue a room with personality—and cost much less than refinishing or replacing it. Prep work is key: Follow the basic guidelines in the first project below for all the rest. A latex enamel paint works best, preferably one formulated for floors and decks.

1 SOLID

Using one bold color makes a big impact. It can also unify the trim and cabinetry in an open floor plan. Fill dents or holes with wood putty; scuff floor with 120-grit sandpaper. Vacuum and wipe with a tack cloth. Add a coat of primer; let dry. Apply two to three coats of paint—you'll want to paint yourself toward the door. Top with two coats of polyurethane for easy cleaning.

2 GRAPHIC

A geometric, tile-like pattern will punch up any kitchen or bathroom. Prep floor (see Solid, left). Paint on base color. When dry, position a paint stencil (sold at crafts stores) in far corner. Dip stencil brush in second color; wipe off excess. Brush over stencil; lift stencil and move to next position. Clean stencil often with running water and a soft brush. Blot dry.

SPLATTER

This Pollock-esque technique works in a nursery, of course, but also a maker space. Prep floor (see Solid, left). Apply two to three coats of base color. Load brush (fine for tiny dots; larger brushes for splotches) with a quarter-inch of paint in second shade; hold brush perpendicular to floor and tap with a dowel so paint spatters. Repeat with a third shade.

RUNNER

Try paint in lieu of a textile stair runner. Dark hues will cover dings better than lighter ones. As here, flank a wider band with different-color stripes for more style points. Prep floor (see Solid, left). Apply two coats of base color (to match wall); let dry. Mark middle swath with painters' tape; paint two coats. Once dry, tape off adjacent strips; paint and let dry.

Wallpaper

Open-Shelf Backdrop

With so many attractive wallpapers to choose from, it can be downright difficult to pick just one. Luckily, a mix of prints can work together beautifully if you stay in the same palette—such as the four cobalt designs used here to line open shelving in a kitchen. (The same idea would work for a bookshelf or china cabinet too.) Remove shelves before applying paper according to manufacturer's instructions (or use self-adhesive paper); when back in place they'll hide the paper's edges, so you don't have to worry about perfect alignment.

Tiered Shelf Liner >

Forget old-school shelf liners—today's self-adhesive wallpaper works as well off the wall as on and comes in pretty patterns, like the speckled terrazzo motif that gives this shelving unit faux-stone appeal. (Imagine how it would look on a tiered coffee table too.) It's also foolproof to apply: Measure the area you want to cover, trim the paper to fit, remove the backing a little at a time, and press to adhere. If it wrinkles, simply peel back a few inches and proceed. If you're concerned about watermarks, top with glass cut to size.

Papered Stair Risers

This wallpaper idea became an instant hit when it first appeared in the magazine (in September 2012!). A single roll will cover a typical stairwell. Apply paper as directed, then protect it with two thin coats of a clear water-based varnish, painting it on with a foam brush.

Lighting

Brass Pendant Lamp

This fixture only looks pricey. It's actually made by repurposing an inexpensive antique-brass bowl from the garden-supply store—be sure to choose one with a thin bottom. Cut a 2-inch hole in the bottom of the bowl with metal snips or nibbler shears, sold at hardware stores. String it upside down with a DIY lamp-cord kit (also in brass and available online) in a cozy reading nook or flanking a sofa.

Dyed-Shade Duo

Two (affordable) lampshades are better than one when bound together to resemble modern rice-paper lanterns. Dye shades in a bath of hot water mixed with fabric dye; let dry. Dot fabric glue such as Magna-Tac 809 around bottom rim of one shade; press other bottom rim against it. Let dry. With a dot of glue, fix end of a center-creased ribbon to the glued center rim. Wrap ribbon all the way around circumference, cut where it overlaps the other end, and secure with another dot of glue. Attach to a floor-lamp base.

Lampshade Liner

Lining a drum shade with gold metallic paper (from an art supply store) casts a warm glow— perfect for a bedroom or a living room.

TOOLS & MATERIALS

Lamp with a drum shade

Metallic foil paper, in gold

Pencil

Scissors or craft knife

Spray adhesive, such as Super 77

1. Detach shade from its base and lay it on its side on the back of the metallic paper. Line up the paper's bottom edge with the shade's, then trace its top edge with a pencil while rolling along the paper; cut with scissors or craft knife.

2. Apply spray adhesive to back of paper and smooth it onto inside of shade; let dry. Reattach the shade to the base.

Textiles

Drapery Headboards >

Whether you buy them or DIY, hanging curtains behind a bed is an elegant way to layer on softness and style. Here, a cheery citrus print (in indoor-outdoor fabric) reinforces the tropical vibe set by the rattan beds and wooden side tables.

THE DETAILS

Basic steel curtain rods with brackets are easy to install out of sight, or use rods with finials for an additional design element. Hang the panels so they just skim the floor and extend a couple of inches beyond the bed on each side. These custom curtains are 66 inches long, but standard 63- or 84-inch ones will also work.

Wooden-Bead Shade Pull

In just half an hour—and for very little money—you can give a pedestrian shade pull a pleasing face-lift. All that's needed is a bunch of chunky (and cheap) crafts-store wooden beads, which you can thread onto the existing cord, knotting at the end to secure. Add additional string for a garland that goes all the way to the floor when the shade is lowered. Tassel not required.

Tip

Use leftover fabric (or buy an extra curtain) to make matching throw-pillow covers.

Curtain Upgrades

Think of a set of plain curtain panels as a blank slate: Customizing them is easy with the following no-sew techniques and basic supplies (including an iron). Natural fibers absorb dyes better than synthetics do, so stick with cotton and linen panels.

1. STAMP: Dip the rim of a glass in a fabric-safe ink pad and press on three or four slightly overlapping circles, then re-ink. Repeat to cover panel.

2. STRIPE: Apply decorative lines to the top portion with iron-on trim, using a variety of widths for visual interest.

3. TINT: Prepare dye and fabric per package instructions. Dip bottom third of panel into dye bath for an ombré effect and hang to air-dry.

4. EDGE: Use iron-on adhesive tape to line inside edge with pom-pom trim. Add a length of plain trim to front to cover seam.

WEEKEND PROJECT

Reversible Linen Curtain

This chic, cord-free window shade is raised by fastening twill-tape loops to shoulder hooks screwed inside the window frame. What makes it genius: using double-face linen, which has a different color (or pattern) on each side. The versatile shade is an affordable alternative to buying custom ones for windows with odd dimensions. Use a tension or café curtain rod for foolproof inside mounting.

TOOLS & MATERIALS

Measuring tape

Double-face linen nylon

Iron

Scissors

Straight pins

Sewing machine

Thread

Sewing needle

Cotton twill tape, ¼ inch

2 solid-brass shoulder hooks

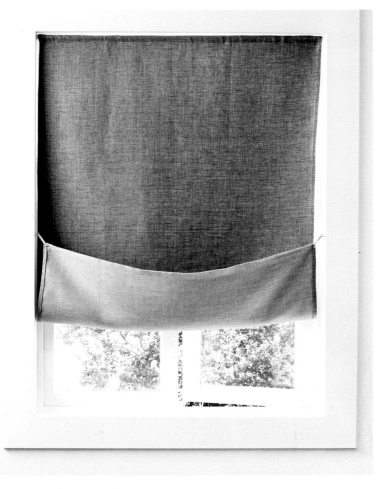

1. Measure width and length of window. Add about 2 inches to allow for hemming at top. For bottom and sides add ½ inch.

2. Wash and dry linen to preshrink it before sewing. Iron smooth. Cut to size.

3. Fold over raw-side edge of linen by ¼ inch; press with iron. Fold over again by a further ¼ inch; press again. Pin, then stitch hem down. Repeat for other side seam and bottom.

4. To make curtain rod pocket, fold over top edge of the linen to the wrong side by ½ inch (for a rod that's ½ inch in diameter); press with iron. Fold over again by another 1½ inches; press again. Pin, then stitch hem down.

5. Cut two 3-inch pieces of twill tape. Double one piece of twill tape and, using a needle and thread, secure loop onto bottom corner of raw side of panel with a few stitches. Repeat on opposite bottom corner.

6. Screw hooks into window frame. Slip curtain loops onto cup hooks to raise shade and reveal contrasting color.

Tip

If you want to let in more light by day, put the screw hooks that hold up the curtain at a higher position.

Quick Quilt

Reinvent a swath of pretty fabric—such as this vintage tablecloth—to make a custom coverlet, like the one featured in the February 2000 issue of *Martha Stewart Living*. You'll also need same-size batting and a larger piece of fabric for the bottom. Pin layers, with fabrics right-side out. Tuft at regular intervals: Send a needle threaded with embroidery floss through layers from top; bring it back up again, $\frac{1}{8}$ inch away. Knot strands together; trim ends. Repeat with two more strands near same spot. Trim bottom fabric to $1\frac{1}{2}$ inches all around. Fold edge over $\frac{1}{2}$ inch; fold it again over top layer; pin. Continue around perimeter. At corners, tuck fabric into itself. Topstitch border in place; hand-stitch corners.

Hand-Stitched Runner

Bound together, four inexpensive 22-by-33-inch rugs become a striking piece that's more than 7 feet long. Use an upholstery needle and thread to whipstitch long sides of two rugs together: Stitch through bottom of first rug, then down through top of second rug, circling back through bottom of first. Knot securely at end of seam. Repeat to attach remaining two rugs.

Stenciled Shower Curtain

When you start with a classic white cotton-duck shower curtain, countless design opportunities await. The smooth weave makes the cloth a foolproof canvas. A polka-dot drop-down wall stencil (sold online) was used to create this playful motif. Use a small pounder to lightly stipple on black fabric paint that can be heat-set with an iron, so it's splashproof.

All-Purpose Upholstery

Outdoor fabrics have moved indoors, thanks to their much-improved look and feel—you can now find them in a slew of pleasing patterns and color palettes. What's more, these durable, weather-resistant textiles can stand up to interior elements (e.g., spilled coffee, sticky fingers, and muddy paws) in high-traffic areas, such as the kitchen. It's the ideal choice if you want to park a sofette next to a table for an instant breakfast nook.

Double Shower Curtains

Two curtains are more luxurious than one (and are better at keeping water inside the tub). Choose all-cotton curtains with graphic patterns for an extra dose of style.

Folding-Screen Headboard

Though its primary purpose is to divvy up rooms, a folding partition can also stand in for a headboard. This upholstered model is plush enough for bedtime reading. Personalize your own screen by having it covered in a handpicked pattern.

Embroidered Throw Pillows

Buy pillows with plain wide-weave covers (like the silk and linen ones shown here) and embellish them yourself, working alpaca yarn right into the weave with a tapestry needle. For bows: Thread needle with 6 to 10 pieces of yarn and pull it through an existing stitch. Trim ends to same length (about 3 inches total); repeat. For stripes: Thread 6 to 10 pieces of yarn through needle. Work it over and under a row of existing stitches. Stop every few inches to tease ends into tufts or change color. For tassels: Thread 10 pieces of yarn through needle. Pull it through a stitch in the side of the pillow, then tie the two ends of yarn in a knot to form a tassel, and trim the ends.

Quilt Wall Art

Why bury a beloved quilt at the foot of a bed or in the linen closet? This striking one is as display-worthy as an abstract painting, while also adding tactile appeal. Quilts can be heavy, however, and may get damaged during hanging. Good news: Wooden quilt hangers (found online) are gentle enough to clasp a vintage specimen or your own handiwork. Some rely on strong magnets to hold together, others have a compression mechanism. Most are inconspicuous and will allow the quilt to remain the star of the show.

Art

Photo Triptych

For a panoramic display, split one grand-scale horizontal image into three vertical panels, then enlarge and hang them in slender frames. When cropping the image, be sure to take the space between frames into account, so the scene flows seamlessly from one to the next.

Tip

To photograph like a pro, start by setting your camera to take and export photos at full resolution. Aim for clean backgrounds, such as a clear blue sky, shimmering body of water, solid bedding, blank wall, or bright window. (For a blown-out, airy effect, tap your phone screen to adjust the exposure.) For the clearest, sharpest prints even when enlarged, use photo files that are 300 pixels per inch (ppi).

Four-Part "Portrait"

So long, staged family photograph. Hello, modern pictorial that makes use of your archives. Choose a quartet of candid images that play together nicely, with different angles, horizon lines, and proportions (zoomed in or out). Convert them to black-and-white to unify the selection and create a timeless tone. Try boosting the contrast too—even sun spots add interest. Hang enlarged photos in a neat grid, using frames in a single bold color like the blue shown here (or natural wood; avoid white or black, as either would be too stark).

Best Practice

PLANNING A GALLERY WALL

It's never amusing to discover, too late, that your art arrangement is crooked or otherwise off-kilter. You can easily avoid that frustration—and all those irksome nail holes—by creating templates, which you can tweak as many times as you like, stepping back to take in the display (all without having someone else holding up disparate pieces). First, trace the picture frames onto kraft paper and cut out the templates. Be sure to label them with the pictures they represent. Pull the hanging wire on the back of each frame taut, and measure from the top of the wire's arc to the upper edge of the frame; this is where the picture hook will go. Then mark this position on the matching template and lay the picture hook on the template so the bottom of the hook is on the mark; make another mark for the nail hole. Then use low-tack painters' or drafting tape to hang the templates on the wall, adjusting them as needed. When you're satisfied with the overall placement, hammer the nails through the picture hooks into wall, right through the marks in the templates. Tear the paper off, leaving nails and hooks in place, and mount your masterpieces.

Painted Frames

When hanging mismatched frames, paint them the same shade to pull them all together. This is also a great way to revive those that have seen better days (such as hand-me-downs and tag-sale finds). Neutral colors, like this light gray, will not detract from the artwork—here set off with creamy mat borders, which also have a unifying effect. Empty frames and cover work surface with kraft paper or newsprint. Go over frame's surface with a wire brush; wipe clean. Then prime (use a tinted primer for darker paints); let dry. Brush on two or three coats of paint, covering top and sides and getting into corners; let dry between coats and before reassembling the refurbished picture frames and hanging.

Space-Saving Display

If your kids generate great quantities of 3D creations (like the string art and clay figurines shown here), snap photos rather than saving every single original—especially if display space is scarce. Set each piece against a contrasting-color backdrop. For the "set": Tape poster board or construction paper to a table or other flat surface; push this against a wall that's hung with more paper. Print photos; put them in simple white frames. Round out the exhibit with other (non-3D) objets d'art.

Tip

Use two different colors or shades as a backdrop to create depth, as with the putty puppy and string sculptures. Also, shoot from different perspectives—above to capture the turtle shells, for example.

Collections

Heirloom Array

Dress up Lucite display cases (the rectangular ones are designed for collectible cereal boxes!) to create a gallery of sentimental artifacts. Linen backing protects the items from dust and unifies the whole set. Trace each frame onto mat board, and cut out the board ¼ inch smaller on all sides to fit neatly inside. Then wrap the board in pretty fabric and tape the edges in back. Mount objects to backing with Velcro hanging strips before fitting them into cases.

Scarf Display

A scarf makes even ho-hum outfits effortlessly chic, and the same can apply to your living spaces. Simply show off the squares in floating acrylic frames and hang them individually, as here, or grouped by color or pattern (such as three behind a sofa or bed). Swap out the wraps for an instant refresh.

Plate Rack Update

Showcase dinnerware in a modern makeshift plate rack. All you need is a shallow wall-mounted shelf (a white model works for this monochromatic scene, or paint an unfinished wood one) and a bold elastic cord, like Paracord Planet's, in lieu of plate stands. Before hanging, drill a hole on each side of the shelf at a height that aligns with center of plates. Thread cord through holes; knot ends.

Basket Arrangement

A grouping of hand-crafted baskets creates a warm welcome on a front porch—or in a guest bedroom or other space you'd like to soften with the woven pieces' natural beauty. So they hang flush with the wall, mount them by driving finishing nails through the middle (rather than the top); the tiny nails won't damage the basket when placed in the weave.

WAYS TO
CREATE TRAVEL KEEPSAKES

Just because your dream vacation is a thing of the past doesn't mean you can't recapture some of that excitement in the future. These four ideas will let you savor—and share—those memories anytime you like by putting them on display. Note to self: Save all those souvenirs!

TREASURE CASE

Corral a curated selection of display-worthy finds and souvenirs from each trip in see-through shadow boxes—gold embellishment optional. Trace the box on a map of where you went, then cut out the map, fit it into bottom of box, and arrange objects on top (glue them in place for shift-free transporting, or leave them free for rummaging and remembering).

TRIP SCRAPBOX

If you're not inclined to painstakingly arrange your memorabilia in a scrapbook, try scrapboxing. Make one keepsake kit for each locale, using a plain hinged wooden box. If desired, brush on one coat of diluted craft paint in a shade of your choice. Let dry, then label: Apply adhesive stencil stickers and daub on letters in contrasting paint with a foam applicator.

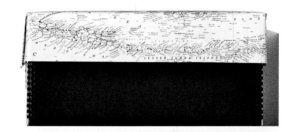

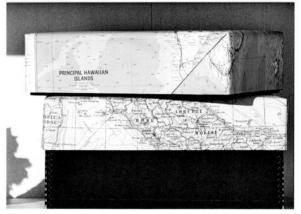

EMBROIDERED ROUTE

Capture your road trips with hand-stitched journeys. Cut map to fit a frame, then poke holes along your route with a needle. Sew along marked path, using a backstitch: Thread needle from back of map through second hole in route; insert needle into first hole, and pull it back out the third. Continue until you reach your destination, then mark it with an X.

MAPPED BOX LID

Another spin on the scrapbox idea, this one uses a map to let you know the getaways at a glance. To wrap the lid of an acid-free box (best for preserving your prized possessions) with a map, first cut map a couple of inches larger than lid, including sides. Then wrap it around lid as you would a gift, tucking in the corners and securing with double-sided tape.

Accents

Colorful Cords

Mirrors in multiples open up a room. These round ones are hung with multicolored cords suspended from cabinet knobs, but any knob or hook will do.

TOOLS & MATERIALS

Mirrors

Paracord (lightweight nylon rope)

Tape measure

Scissors

Knobs and hardware, for hanging

1. For an 8-inch-diameter mirror, cut an 80-inch piece of paracord; fold in half. (Add 2 inches of cord for every additional inch in diameter.)

2. Tie a basic knot 13 inches from folded end to form a loop. (Add 1 inch for every additional inch in diameter.) Lay mirror down, reflective-side up; place cord loop on top, with knot near lower end.

3. Bring loose cord ends to back of mirror. Thread through loop at top; pull tight to prevent slippage. Spread apart cord on front to form an upside-down V.

4. Tie a basic knot a few inches from end; hang from an anchor-secured knob.

⟨ Instant Entryway

The quickest way to lend style and substance to a foyer or kid's room? Hang up colorful hooks to punctuate a patterned wallpaper. Find hangers in fun shapes, like these oversized circles, and paint them to match your palette. Be sure to arrange them at a variety of heights so everyone can reach!

Vertical Gardening

Plants can double as cheerful wall décor when placed on bright brackets in a room with good natural light. Arrange brackets in desired pattern on the floor, then measure and mark spots on the wall. Screw brackets into studs or secure with plastic wall anchors. For drip-free displaying, nestle each potted plant in a larger, hole-less pot and carry the inner pots to the sink to water; let plants drain well before returning to their perches.

Easy Plant Stands

Metal tomato cages are inexpensive and can be found at any nursery or home improvement center. Here they go from utilitarian to ornamental plant holders with just a few steps. Invert them and cut off just their feet (right) or, for more stability, cut them to a shorter height (left)—recommended for heavier plants. Spray-paint the cages gold, as we did, or any shade you like. Then find decorative pots that fit inside securely.

Stitched Screen Address

Upgrade your screen door by stitching on your address number—the existing mesh grid is a foolproof guide. This idea was inspired by one of the crafts in *You Are Awesome*, by Abbey Hendrickson.

TOOLS & MATERIALS

Adhesive number stencils (optional)
Chalk
Colorful nylon twine
Tapestry needle, size 18
Match

1. Affix stencils onto screen; trace with chalk (or draw freehand).

2. Thread a few feet of twine into the needle; knot. (Melt ends of twine with a lit match to keep from fraying.)

3. Starting at a corner of each number, insert needle from back of screen and pull through. Push needle back into screen at next corner. Continue with stitches on alternating sides of screen until you reach the starting point. Then stitch entire number again, so thread appears as a continuous line. Knot cord and melt end.

Rock Door Stops

Use Plasti Dip—sold at hardware stores to give tool grips a bright, slip-proof coating—to turn any sizable stone into a handy, scratch-free doorstop. Cover top half of rock with masking tape and submerge the other half a few times into a paper bowl of Plasti Dip to coat completely. Let rock dry and peel off tape before putting it to work.

Stenciled Dining Chairs

Assigned seating, made easy: Starting with the middle letter of each person's name, affix adhesive stencils to center of chair backs. Working outward, fill in letters with contrasting-color craft paint and a stencil brush, then let paint dry.

Tip

Flip chairs onto a drop cloth for more stable stenciling.

Towel Rings

Encourage little ones to wash—and dry—their hands by mounting kids' wooden gymnastics rings (found online) to the wall of their bathroom, for easy hand-towel access. For each one, loop a 1½-inch-wide leather strap (these are about 10 inches long) through a ring, then punch holes ½ inch above the ring using a leather punch, and secure with a screw-in foot. To hang, punch a hole in the back strip and mount using a wall anchor and screw. Stagger them on the wall so they are within easy reach.

WEEKEND PROJECT

Wooden-Bead Trivet

Here's a nifty way to use up an excess stash of wooden craft beads (or a good excuse to pick up new ones). Paint some beads in your desired palette, or keep them all natural. Set aside a few hours to make multiple trivets, assembly-line fashion, for keeping (and displaying) or gifting.

TOOLS & MATERIALS

Craft paint
Paintbrush
Wooden beads, in assorted sizes
Leather cord, about 2 feet long

1. Paint all but largest beads (direct heat may wear away the color); let dry 1 hour. String onto cord, alternating between large and small sizes. Adjust trivet size by adding or removing beads.

2. Tie cord ends together tightly so beads form a ring; trim excess, or tie it into a loop to hang on a hook.

Dyed Tea Towels

Ditch the disposable napkins! Dye pellets from a crafts store make it easy to turn white cotton dish towels bought by the dozen into colorful, reusable versions. Follow package directions to dye the towels—do it in batches, one shade at a time—in the washing machine, then tumble dry to set the tint.

Tableware Storage
and Care, PAGE 55

2

Homekeeping

Your living space and belongings should bring
you pleasure—not weigh you down. The following pages are
chock-full of hints to make common chores—from
dishes to laundry—that much more manageable. You'll find an
eco-friendly ethos here that focuses on preserving
what you already own and eschewing harsh chemicals. So get
inspired to raid the pantry for all-natural cleaners and
pesticides, mend tired sweaters to give them a
new personality, and nurture houseplants so they thrive—
then sit back and enjoy your home.

Cleaning

Cast-Iron Upkeep

A well-seasoned cast-iron skillet (see page 135) is a cook's best friend—it's naturally nonstick and goes from stovetop to oven (to table). But stubborn residue can build up over time. Common practice is to rub the surface with a paste of coarse salt and hot water. When it gets heavy, the solution is thorough cleaning and reseasoning. Doing so usually involves heating (and possibly smoking) up the house with a very hot oven, but here's a way to clean it when cooking over a campfire—or when otherwise using a firepit or fireplace. Put the skillet in hot ashes after the fire has died out. Let it cool completely, then wipe pan with a wet dishcloth and reseason.

Easy Copper Care

Your copper pots, pans, and serving pieces require regular polishing to look their best. There are a number of metal-specific creams you can buy, but you might have the remedy you need right in your kitchen: Rub copper with a cut lemon sprinkled with salt until it gleams, then rinse with lukewarm water and dry with a clean cloth. Ketchup happens to contain enough vinegar to remove tarnish; rub it on with your hands and let it sit a few minutes, then rinse and dry.

Drain Deodorizer

There's an easy way to avoid having a stinky kitchen sink: Pour 1 cup baking soda followed by ¼ cup distilled white vinegar down the drain. Let this bubble away for 15 minutes, then flush with running hot tap water. Doing this regularly—monthly or as needed—will also help prevent clogs from forming. (Keeping grease out of the sink, and using a stopper to keep food bits from washing down, will also help.) If you have an automatic garbage disposal, pulverize a lemon half every now and then to remove odors from that too.

CLASSIC GOOD THING

Soap Dispenser

Your sparkling kitchen sink is a sight to behold. Or, it would be, if not for the plastic bottle by its side. The solution: Decant dishwashing liquid into an attractive glass bottle and cap it with a pour spout (introduced in the April/May 1993 issue of *Martha Stewart Living*). You'll also save money by buying the soap in bulk and the planet by avoiding unnecessary packaging. The same goes for transferring hand soap to pretty vessels for all your bathroom sinks.

DIY Cleaners

You don't need a bunch of pricey single-use store-bought formulas to get your home sparkling. Instead, make your own eco-friendly solutions using basic pantry items. Add a few drops of essential oil (such as lemon, lavender, or rosemary) for an all-natural scent.

ALL-PURPOSE SPRAY: ½ cup vinegar + 2 cups water + 2 drops essential oil

GLASS SPRAY: one part vinegar + one part water

DRAIN DECLOGGER: ½ cup baking soda + ½ cup vinegar + boiling water (plug drain for 15 minutes after adding vinegar and before flushing with boiling water)

OVEN CLEANER: three parts warm water + one part baking soda

CUTTING BOARD/BUTCHER BLOCK DEODORIZER: ½ lemon + coarse salt (dip cut side to coat)

STAINLESS STEEL CLEANER: equal parts baking soda and water (apply with a damp cloth; rinse and buff dry)

Best Practice

10 MORE WAYS TO USE VINEGAR

1. CLEAN THE COFFEE MAKER: Run a brew cycle using vinegar; rinse with two cycles of water before brewing coffee.

2. CLEAN THE MICROWAVE: Put a bowl of vinegar in unit; cook on high for 1 minute, then wipe down surfaces.

3. ADD TO THE DISHWASHER: Use as a rinse agent instead of store-bought formulas; also run an empty machine with a cup of vinegar on the upper rack to clean it.

4. ADD TO WASH LOADS: Pour in ½ cup vinegar during rinse cycle to remove mildew in towels, brighten colors and whites, and soften fabric (but never mix with bleach).

5. DISINFECT BATH TOYS: Once a month, soak toys in warm, soapy water with ½ cup vinegar for 15 minutes, scrubbing nooks with a toothbrush. Rinse well.

6. DESCALE FAUCETS/SHOWERHEADS: Tie a vinegar-filled plastic bag around spigot. Leave at least 15 minutes or preferably overnight. Scrub with a toothbrush.

7. TACKLE WATER MARKS ON WOOD: Apply equal parts vinegar and olive oil to stain with a white cloth, wiping with the grain. Repeat as needed.

8. DISINFECT SCISSORS AND GARDEN PRUNERS: Water can lead to rust, so wipe blades with a rag dampened in vinegar instead.

9. KEEP CUT FLOWERS ALIVE: Mix 3 tablespoons sugar, 2 tablespoons vinegar, and 4 cups warm water; let cool and use in the vase, covering stems by at least 3 inches.

10. KILL WEEDS: Mix 1 gallon vinegar, 1 cup salt, and 1 tablespoon dishwashing soap; spray on problem spots. Repeat as needed. (Do not do if rain is in the forecast.)

Tableware Storage and Care

Follow these general tips to keep your china-cabinet finery looking its best. Crystal, china, and silver should be washed only by hand—remove any jewelry first. Rub off lipstick stains from glasses with a vinegar-soaked cotton ball. When stacking delicate china, protect it by inserting paper plates between plates and bowls. Clean silver in warm, soapy water after each use (before oxidation sets in); rub any wood accents with beeswax. To remove excess tarnish, polish pieces with silver-specific cream (such as Wright's or Hagerty) and a soft cloth, using a cotton swab to reach into nooks and crannies. Avoid baking soda baths, which can be damaging. Store silver pieces in their original cloth bags to help prevent future tarnish—or at least line the shelf (or drawer) with extra linens, which will also protect against scratches and scrapes.

CLASSIC GOOD THING

Portable Cleaning Station

Streamline your weekly cleaning routine with this grab-and-go system that appeared in the April 2002 issue of *Martha Stewart Living*. Simply stock a handy pail with these essentials: all-purpose and glass-cleaning sprays (see left for make-your-own versions), sponges (one for sinks and tubs, another for toilets), a scrub brush, an old toothbrush, lint-free cloths, and a pair of rubber gloves—hang those over the rim to dry.

Slip-Proof Kitchen Towel

The oven-door pull is a convenient place to hang a towel—it is within easy reach and dries more quickly from the oven's heat. But it also tends to slide off whenever you open the door or neglect to put it back just so. Keep it in place by joining both ends to make a loop, securing with iron-on (or stitched) Velcro strips—one on the front and one on the back. This also lets you rotate the towel to keep a dry section facing out.

Dish-Soap Savings

Take a cue from restaurants when cleaning a sinkful of dirty pots and dishes with fewer suds: Rather than constantly adding dishwashing soap to each item, squirt a small amount of the liquid into a plastic quart container (the kind you get from a takeout dinner) or other scratch-proof vessel, fill it with warm water, and keep it in the sink. Then dip your cleaning brush in this as you go, replenishing as needed.

Vase-Cleaning Tips ❯

Cleaning vases and other flower repositories can be a tricky task. To remove stubborn water lines from a glass vessel, fill it with vinegar to above the line; let sit for a few hours, then loosen stains with a bottle brush, rinse well, and dry with a lint-free cloth. Small-necked bottles can be especially challenging: Fill them with water, drop in a tablet or two of a denture cleanser (such as Efferdent), and let stand overnight. Scrub with a narrow nylon brush; rinse and dry.

Tub and Tile Routine

Bathrooms can get gritty fast. With all the toxic cleansers being used, consider rotating in some efficient natural scouring formulas: Mix 1 teaspoon of liquid soap and several drops of an antibacterial essential oil (such as tea tree, eucalyptus, rosemary, or peppermint) with 1 cup of baking soda. Add just enough water to form a paste, and apply it with a sponge or brush to bathtub surfaces (including tiles), then rinse to reveal their sparkle and shine.

Scented Wreath

You might not think to hang a wreath in the bathroom. But when it's made with fresh, fragrant greenery, it's more than décor—the shower's steam helps release its invigorating scent. Plus, the leafy herbs will dry as they hang, so the display has staying power. This one is made by securing a branch of seeded eucalyptus with wire. You could also bundle bunches of fresh rosemary or bay laurel, or a combination.

Dust-Free Fireplace Cleaning

Here's an easy way to "ground out" the dust, and keep the mess to a minimum, when clearing away spent fireplace ashes: Simply save your used coffee grounds each time you brew; when ready to clean the hearth, dampen them and scatter them evenly over the ashes. They'll make everything easier to scoop and prevent the ashes from polluting the room with all that airborne dust. Safety reminder: Always let the ashes cool completely before removing.

Laundering

Pet Hair Removal

Instead of investing in lots of specialty tools that promise to keep the fur from flying, why not employ a few items from your existing arsenal? Rubber is a magnet for pet hair—run a cleaning glove or squeegee across low-pile rugs and upholstery between weekly vacuumings. And for an easy layer of protection, put an old towel in your pet's favorite lounging spot (shake it outside before laundering in hot water).

Seasonal Bedding

If you have a soft spot for pretty quilts and printed sheets, don't just tuck them away between uses. Enlist a side chair to hold a curated selection, where it can be seen and enjoyed, swapping it out as the seasons change. You'll want neat folds: For thicker comforters, fold each side one-third of the way, then lengthwise; fold corners of thinner coverlets toward the center, on the bias.

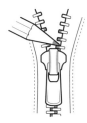

Zipper Fixers

Next time you find yourself with a stuck zipper (it's inevitable), grap a pencil (a soft graphite "artist" pencil is best). Color the teeth of the zipper completely on both sides with the lead point, then give the zipper a tug. If that doesn't do the trick, experiment with other household lubricants—bar soap, dishwashing soap, clear lip balm, talc or baby powder, and glass cleaner are all fair game.

Smooth Sheets

Ironing is still the only way to achieve ultra-crisp results, but here's a nifty workaround that comes close: Toss a few ice cubes into the dryer with your bedsheets; the ice will melt during the cycle and create steam. Take the sheets out when just dry, hang them up, and snap the fabric a few times until remaining wrinkles release. This method works best with smaller loads—launder linens for one bed at a time.

Tip

You can also quickly smooth out wrinkles once sheets are on the bed with a garment steamer—it's a secret technique of photo stylists.

Sweater Repairs

If your favorite knitwear is showing its age, give it an instant refresh with these simple solutions.

1. To defuzz, gently run a fine-tooth comb over the sweater's surface; it will catch pills without harming the garment.

2. To fix a snag, push a small crochet hook from the inside of the sweater out and catch the yarn. Then pull it back through the same spot until it's hidden on the inside.

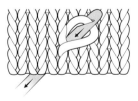

Stain Chart

When it first appeared in the magazine in January 2004, this chart set the standard as the go-to resource for tackling spills and stains, and it's as useful today as ever. You can photocopy the chart on pages 276–277. Then slide it into a clear plastic sleeve (or have it laminated at a print shop) and suspend it from a clamp hanger in your laundry area. This way you'll know how to treat the common culprits (coffee, mud, lipstick) at a glance.

Waterproofed Outdoor Apparel

With a fabric-wax bar (such as Otter Wax, sold online), you can improve the performance and extend the life of canvas goods and give them a vintage look in the process. Start with an item that's free of dirt and dust. Test in an inconspicuous spot to see if you like it (fabric will darken and take on an aged patina), then work bar evenly into canvas, scrubbing quickly and pressing with your fingers to spread the wax. Use the bar's edges to get into seams; remove excess with a toothpick. Let it cure for 72 hours before wearing.

DIY Dryer Balls

Wool dryer balls are reusable, nontoxic, all-natural alternatives to dryer sheets and fabric softeners. They help separate and aerate clothes as they dry, reducing static, wrinkling, and drying time, so they save on energy costs. Making your own is easy—and a good way to use up a leftover ball of yarn (choose one that is at least 80 percent wool). Tuck the yarn into the toe of a pair of nylons. Run it through the hottest cycles of the washer and dryer a few times until it's dense and bouncy. It will last for years.

Crease-Free Linens

Keeping your table linens wrapped around cardboard tubes when not in use will ensure they're always ready for a party. Use a mailing/poster tube for tablecloths and runners, paper-towel rolls for dinner napkins, and bathroom-tissue tubes for cocktail napkins. Store them in a linen closet or a sideboard drawer.

Dry-Cleaning Alternatives

A label that says "dry-clean only" doesn't always mean you can't safely clean the item at home. In fact, doing so can save money and preserve your garments (harsh chemicals take a toll over time). Try these methods:

WOOL SWEATERS: Hand-wash in cool water with wool-safe detergent, such as Woolite; reshape garment on a towel, then roll up and gently squeeze (never wring) to remove excess water. Lay flat to dry.

PREMIUM DENIM: Turn jeans and jackets inside out and machine-wash them in cold water on the delicate cycle. Shake out wrinkles and hang them to dry.

SILK BLOUSES: Hand-wash, adding all-natural fabric softener to soak. Hang dry, and steam or iron.

Tip — Max out your air-drying space by installing a ceiling-mounted rack.

Whiter Summer Whites

There are a few ways to launder whites to keep them clean and bright throughout the season: Add ½ cup borax or ¼ cup white vinegar to the laundry, or boil water with lemon halves in a large pot, then soak your linens until the water is cool. When it's time for long-term winter storing, keep these garments in boxes made of breathable cotton; avoid cardboard, which contains acid that can yellow white fabric over time.

On-the-Spot Solution

The key to successfully removing any stain is to treat it as soon as possible. Hanging a mini kit in a hamper (this one rests over the rim) will help ensure you address those soiled items before they get buried in a pile of dirty laundry. Stock the kit with a small bottle of acetone (for removing grass and grease), diluted dish soap (for red wine, tomato sauces, and blood), and white vinegar (great on mustard, coffee, and tea). Include a soft-bristled brush for stubborn spots.

WAYS TO

MEND GARMENTS

Adopt a fix-it-don't-toss-it approach to your wardrobe with these artful amendments, aka "visible mending." With only beginner sewing skills and basic supplies, you can patch tears, darn holes, reinforce a buttonhole, or fix a pulled thread—and give a tired piece new personality to boot.

PATCH A TEAR

Embrace the Japanese tradition of *sashiko* ("little stabs") whenever you're faced with a tear. Unlike old-school knee patches, with this method the placket goes on the inside and graphic stitching decorates the outside. Pin placket in place. Thread an embroidery needle with contrasting-color thread and create decorative lines using a running stitch.

REINFORCE A BUTTONHOLE

Refortify a loose buttonhole by adding a nifty patch to the placket—this striped one perks up otherwise plain chambray. Then cover the hole's edges with closely placed blanket stitches for a pop of color. The bright rows of running stitches mask a rip in the pocket that's fortified with an interior patch, for another example of *sashiko* (left).

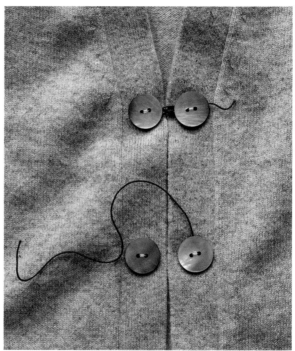

MASK FRAYING

If your knitwear is looking threadbare, accentuate worn-out areas with simple abstract stitches in bold shades. Note how even the brighter yellow thread stands out amidst the fuchsia. Make sure the thread is of a similar thickness and material; a thin mohair yarn blends nicely with this fuzzy vest.

REPLACE BUTTONS

If your cardigan is missing a button (or even if not), give it a top-down update with buttons on both sides and a cord closure (à la an interoffice envelope). Stitch buttonholes closed; remove buttons. Sew on even pairs of new buttons. Cut 10 inches of elastic cord in a vivid hue for each set; tie on behind buttons on one side. Loop and crisscross cord back and forth to secure shut.

Gardening

Indoor Potting "Bench"

For a convenient, mess-free way to care for houseplants, follow the lead of *Martha Stewart Living* garden editors by using a large shallow bin as a portable workstation and storage solution in one. Stock it with all the necessary supplies—such as extra pots, stakes, plant labels, pruners, potting mix, and gravel. Then empty it out and do your repotting and fertilizing right inside it (no more spilled soil to vacuum up). Simply dump it outside after each use, sweeping it clean with a handbroom.

Plant Binder

Even experienced gardeners need help remembering how to care for different plants—and a system for keeping track of all their instructive tags. A small expandable file (like this pretty green one, which appeared in the May 2015 issue of *Martha Stewart Living*) from an office-supply store can be your go-to guide; just slip plant info in pockets organized by location.

Living Wreath

Ferns are popular as houseplants—and make beautiful wreaths too. Cover a wreath form with sphagnum moss. Divide a fern into mini plants, keeping roots attached; tuck stems into moss to anchor plantlets as they grow. Use a variety of ferns, as here, for more visual interest. Hang wreath indoors, following the plant tag's instructions for access to natural light, and mist occasionally.

Vacation Plant Care

Plants, just like pets, call for their own breed of TLC while you are away. Make sure house sitters are clear on what needs to be done, and when. Print a note for each pot, including watering guidelines and any other instructions—like rotating every so often for even sunlight. Then stick the cards into the soil with wooden markers (or chopsticks).

Weed Decoder

Rethink your disdain for weeds—they might be nuisances, but they can tell you a lot about the state of your soil. Check the categories below for familiar culprits (search online for images). Once you know what's growing—and have pulled out the offenders—you can take steps to amend the soil (consult your local cooperative extension for guidance) and help your desired plants thrive.

WET: Curly dock, buttercup, horsetail, smartweed, bull sedge, jewelweed

COMPACTED: Chicory, bindweed, burdock, field mustard

ACIDIC: Dandelion, mullein, stinging nettle, cinquefoil, hawkweed

ALKALINE: Nodding thistle, stinkweed, pennycress

NUTRIENT-POOR: Wild parsnip, sheep sorrel, henbit, dog fennel

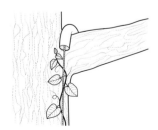

Climbing-Plant Support

Clematis, hydrangea, passionflower—these and other slow climbers can make your taller trees look even more attractive. Problem is, the necessary supports pose the risk of damaging the branches they cling to. Protect these limbs (and your tree's health) by placing the supporting twine or wire inside pieces cut from a retired garden hose. Black rubber will blend into the bark, green into the foliage.

Hanging Herb Garden

How's this for a smart repurpose: Fill a hanging mesh basket not with different fruits (its intended purpose) but with a vertical herb "garden." The three tiers pack a lot of produce in a slim space—whether on a balcony, porch, or backyard. Bonus: It'll be protected from common ground pests and critters. To grow your own, line each basket with sphagnum moss, which helps keep the soil moist, fill with organic potting soil, and plant with your favorite herbs (basil, mint, and sage are shown here). Hang it in a sunny spot, and water it whenever the soil feels dry.

Seed Bombs

These mixed-seed marvels are a quick way to plant a wildflower patch—and a fun activity for kids. They also happen to make great gifts that keep on giving. Mix together five parts natural air-drying clay (from a crafts store), one part compost, and one part seeds (4 ounces will cover up to 500 square feet). Using native plants will best support your local pollinators, so ask your garden center for suggestions. Roll into 1-inch balls and dry on waxed paper for a few days. Toss them in an area that's free of grass or weeds after the last frost date (on a still day); water regularly.

Natural Pest Control

Don't let critters—or unpleasant fumigating—ruin your outdoor enjoyment. These all-natural repellents will rid your favorite spaces of unwanted visitors without any harsh chemicals.

ORANGE-OIL DEFENSE: To get rid of ants, dampen a cotton swab with a few drops of orange essential oil, then wipe it on a porch or patio perimeter (or table and chair legs).

PEPPERMINT-OIL DETERRENT: To repel spiders, ants, and aphids in one fell swoop, add 10 to 15 drops of peppermint essential oil to a spray bottle of water and spritz on problem areas, including plants.

NEST DECOY: To ward off wasps, try fashioning a faux hive so the territorial stingers will build their nest elsewhere. Inflate a brown paper lunch bag, draw on details with a black marker, and hang it upside down on your porch or other protected spot in the yard.

Storing Fresh Herbs

Just-picked herbs are much more likely to languish when stored in the refrigerator. They're also too pretty to hide away. Instead, keep bunches on the kitchen countertop where you can appreciate their aroma—and easily clip what you need at any time. Rinse the stems before grouping in a vessel, mixing different herbs for visual interest and varied flavor profiles. When planning your herb garden, start with the types you use most often, like thyme and rosemary, and then work in less common ones you want to try, such as shiso.

Leaf-Mold Mulch

Here's a good reason to save your raked leaves in the fall—the mulch you can make with them will improve the quality of your soil and help it retain moisture. You'll also save money by not having to purchase wood chips or other mulches. Collect leaves in a jute sack or plastic trash bag, spray them with water, and close the bag. (If using plastic, poke a few holes in the bag.) Then put it in a cool, shady spot; the leaves will decompose in about a year. Spread the mulch in your garden as needed.

Smart Bulb Storage

For a "green" way to store tender bulbs like dahlias, tuberoses, cannas, and elephant ears over the winter, reach for a file box. Place the bulbs in the container and fill with shredded paper from your home office; the shreds will absorb moisture and keep the bulbs from touching. Keep in a cool, dark, and dry place until you're ready to plant in the spring.

Pinecone Bird Feeder

Put fallen pinecones to use as all-natural feeders. This is a fun and easy project for kids:

1. Spread peanut butter on a cone's scales.

2. Pour birdseed mix into a shallow bowl. Roll the pinecone in the mix until covered. Loop twine around the top of the pinecone and hang it from a tree.

Companion Planting for Vegetable Gardens ⟩

Make the most of your space and your efforts with this age-old technique of growing certain vegetables and herbs together for mutually beneficial purposes: soil condition, sun requirements, pest and weed control, climbing support, and more. Here are some classic groupings.

TOMATOES/EGGPLANTS/PEPPERS + HERBS + BORAGE: Nightshades must be planted after the last threat of frost has passed. Edge the beds with herbs that like the same growing conditions, such as basil and parsley. Borage can also help keep away destructive tomato hornworms (and its periwinkle flowers taste like cucumber).

POTATOES + BEANS: Plant seed potatoes in spring, after the soil thaws. Beans on poles or trellises make friendly upstairs neighbors, enriching the soil with nitrogen. The two plants help deter pests that are known to plague the other.

CORN + SQUASH + BEANS: Native Americans call these complementary plants the "three sisters": Corn grows on a tall stalk, providing a natural support for beans, and beans return the favor by adding nourishing nitrogen to the soil. Squash grows happily beneath the other two, helping to keep weeds down and soil moist.

RADISHES + CARROTS: Let these roots mingle in the same row. They thrive in cooler temperatures, so start them early. After radishes sprout and you pull them up, there will be more room for the slower-growing carrots.

CUCUMBERS + PEAS: Like beans, peas and cucumbers climb while they grow, so train them to fences and trellises. Start peas as soon as you can work the soil, then add cucumbers later, after the last frost.

KALE + SWISS CHARD: These leafy greens will thrive together in the same bed, and both grow easily and quickly from seed. Spinach (a relative of chard) is another option here. Sow in early spring and continue to grow through fall.

Fall Hanging Baskets

Come autumn, swap out your spent summer flowers with cold-hardy plants, such as the ornamental cabbage and kale shown here. Arranged over a base of Spanish moss, these bountiful plantings will lend seasonal beauty to your outdoor spaces.

Lawn Care

Watering is a must to keep your summer lawn looking its best. Overdoing it, however, wastes money and goes against a conservation ethos. So the answer is to water only when the grass is truly thirsty. How to gauge that? Walk across the yard: If you can see your footprints, it's time to turn on the sprinkler, preferably a pulsating one for the most even coverage. This type also sends water where it is most beneficial, meaning down to the roots.

Tool Grips

Adhesive handlebar tape (such as S-Wrap Roubaix or Cinelli Cork Ribbon) comes in bright shades and makes wooden tools slip-proof and more comfortable. Tightly wrap handle from bottom to top, overlapping slightly, then wrap tape around itself, trim, and press to secure.

Tip

Watering the lawn—and your garden beds—deeply as needed is better than daily light soaks. For beds, wait until the top 2 inches of soil feel dry before drenching. Always water early in the day to reduce risk of fungal disease.

Entryway Cabinet,
PAGE 81

3

Organizing

Make every room work harder—that's what the
unexpected strategies on these pages promise to do. They target
all the usual problem spots without relying on same-old
solutions. Think upcycling and repurposing before cluttering
with more stuff: a charming bike basket for housing
garden tools, perhaps, and pretty bowls for sorting jewelry
and cosmetics. Employ everyday items in new ways to
expand storage: file folders in a kitchen cabinet? You bet. Another
very good thing: Color-code everything, from cooking tools
to bathroom supplies, for orderly bliss.

Entryway

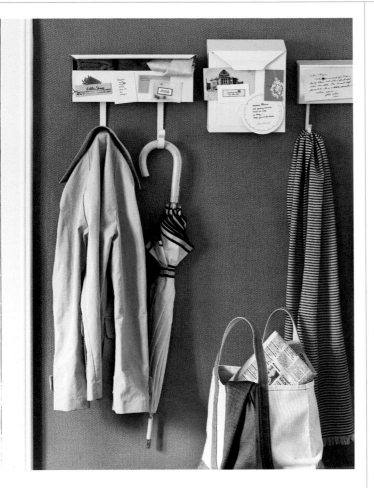

Paper-Roll Message "Board"

If you're looking for a more original, and space-saving, take on the traditional memo board, give a roll of drawing paper a new spin. String a strip of leather through the roll, duct-tape the ends together (and hide that part inside the roll), then hang the strip from a wall-mounted hook. To anchor the paper, ask your local hardware store to cut an aluminum angle an inch wider than the paper and make a hole on either end; drill screws through holes into your wall.

Magnetic Hall Organizer

Metal mailboxes—specifically the wall-mounted kinds meant for apartment lobbies and front porches—can be multitasking marvels in an entry or mudroom. Besides managing mail, the boxes are roomy enough to stash hats, gloves, and other seasonal sundries. Those with hooks can also hold coats and umbrellas. And they're magnetic, so you can tack up notes, photos, and postcards. To unify the look, spray-paint the boxes white or in a color that matches your trim.

Easy-Access Sports Station

Create an all-in-one spot for active kids' gear—and reclaim your house. Start with a standard-issue shelving unit, and sort items into different wire or plastic bins. A clip-on basket makes use of under-shelf space. Drill holes into two shelves to anchor bungee-cord hooks to keep a bevy of balls in place.

WEEKEND PROJECT

Entryway Cabinet

Make this DIY console by placing two unfinished wood cabinets side by side and painting them a soft green (or your desired shade) inside and out.

TO OPTIMIZE STORAGE

- Add wooden legs (or mount cabinets on wall) so there's room underneath.

- Stick self-adhesive hooks inside doors; adjust shelves (these came with two each) to accommodate different items.

- Assign a cubby to each family member or purpose—scarves and bags, petkeeping supplies, and mail, for example.

CLASSIC GOOD THING

Better Boot Tray

Putting a tray inside entrances protects floors from dripping boots and shoes. For a harder-working—and better-looking—solution (like this one from *Martha Stewart Living*, January 2006), fill the container with pebbles or stones from a garden center. They'll serve as drains, allowing rain, sleet, and snow to seep to the bottom, leaving your footwear to dry. Most of the moisture will evaporate, but do regular cleanouts to keep the tray fresh.

Modular Shelving

Try this adaptable arrangement in a space-challenged foyer—it's hall closet, command center, and minimalist décor all in one. You can replicate the design shown here or add more shelves or pegs to suit your situation and family needs. Start by cutting 10-inch dowels to match the shelf's depth (these are 8 inches). Paint just the ends of the pegs to add small pops of color; let dry. Screw them into the wall (using appropriate anchoring hardware) at even intervals— each of these pairs is 16 inches apart to accommodate 24-inch-long shelves. Screw 5-inch dowels (also painted) below the shelves to hang umbrellas, scarves, and bags. What makes this system even more practical is how it can be adapted over time. Remove a shelf to make room for coats in winter; add a lower shelf to accommodate sunglasses and SPF in summer. Park a bench for seating and storage underneath, and the entry's all set.

Staircase Storage

Under-stair spaces are often wasted. For this custom built-in, have a carpenter carve the wall into equal heights, add drawer bottoms and handles to middle section, and leave lower slot open for supplies or a place to store shoes.

Bulletin Board Makeover

Wrap a simple magnet board in a favorite fabric and voilà! It's instantly pretty enough to keep in the entry as a family message center. Stretch a piece of cloth (a colorful pattern ties all the rest together) over the board, and staple it to the back.

Kitchen

Driftwood Shelf

Bring a nautical vibe—and sneaky under-shelf storage—to a kitchen (or bathroom) by threading a driftwood branch through open wall brackets. Drape towels over the limb, or use leather strips to hang items such as the cutting board and pitcher shown here.

Tip

Group items on a pantry shelf into zones—for instance, tea service, decanted dry goods, food-prep supplies, and storage vegetables in open bins.

File-Folder Dividers

It's such a nuisance digging out a muffin tin or cutting board from the bottom of a pile. Instead, stand these oft-used items up in wire dividers from an office-supply store. A shorter cabinet, above the oven or refrigerator, is just the place to do this.

Open Pantry

No room for a real larder? Coat a steel shelving unit with metal-specific spray paint. Decant items into pretty crocks, jars, and bins. Slip brass S hooks and wooden dowels into the rivet holes to hold pans, butcher twine, and other kitchen supplies.

Pot Organizer

This idea from *Martha Stewart Living*'s January 2012 issue gives each pan its own "shelf," as opposed to nesting. You can grab the pan you need, with just one free hand! Use cable clips to secure a bakeware organizer, turned on its end, to one wall of your cabinet. Sort cookware by size, largest on the bottom.

Pull-Out Inserts

These sliding space savers can double the storage of deep cabinets. They also let you reach items in the back without having to take everything out. They're available at home improvement centers (and online) in wood or metal and in a range of sizes to fit standard cabinets. Measure and mark the sides of yours, factoring in the height of the items to be stored there; use a drill to attach the glides, then pop in the drawers.

Staples Station

A lazy Susan lets you corral most-used items near your cooktop—just spin to reach what you need. A variety of sea salts and fresh-ground pepper (and a favorite seasoning blend) in coordinating dishes make for easy pinching as you work.

Pot-Lid Sorter

These kitchen essentials can be irksome to store—especially if you hang your pots and pans, which preempts you from keeping the lids atop their matching bases. Instead, use screws to mount a rubber-coated storage rack sold just for this purpose inside the door of a base cabinet, and the lids will always be within easy reach.

Trash-Bag Storage

Get rid of bulky boxes and keep track of your supply level with this one neat trick: Hang rolls of trash and recycling bags inside the under-sink cabinet door. Cut a ½-inch-diameter dowel slightly longer than bag's width. Screw a set of ¾-inch curtain-rod brackets from the hardware store (brass ones look especially nice) into inside of door. Slide roll of bags onto dowel, then suspend it from brackets.

Cup-and-Saucer Stack

This tip for safely storing your teacups has been a *Martha Stewart Living* classic since September 2006. Instead of nestling the saucers in one neat pile and the cups in a teetering stack, arrange them in matching sets, one atop another. This method looks tidy, protects against chipping, and makes it easier to grab a pair in one fell swoop, saving time when entertaining.

Kid-Friendly Drawer

Give kids a low-enough kitchen drawer, and they'll be more likely to do for themselves come snack- or mealtime. Use dividers and shallow bins to group by category and keep items from colliding when opening and closing the drawer. And create an assigned space for everything, to encourage kids to put things back too. A painted silhouette of each type of vessel (like the dinner plates shown here) in a bold color works well for pre-readers; be sure to write or stencil on a label, as well.

Cabinet Expanders

How often do you wish you had just one more cabinet? Installing an extra one likely isn't an option in an already tight space. But wire risers, sold at housewares stores, are an affordable way to make the most of what you have. They're expandable too, so they'll fit any dimension. Put a couple side by side to span an entire shelf and/or to separate types of drinkware.

Color-Coded Tools

Wooden boards and utensils can take on the flavors and smells of the foods they're used for. Clearly mark each of a set of identical boards with a strip of acrylic paint—one color for raw meats (for food safety), one for fruit, and one for vegetables. Do the same for utensils. Tape around strip for neat lines; avoid painting surfaces that touch food.

Wall-Mounted System

Why buy when you can easily DIY a minimalist storage system that makes the most of vertical space in a (small) kitchen? The slim racks, made by slipping painted dowels into brass brackets, are just right for housing pot lids, utensils, and other lightweight items.

TOOLS & MATERIALS

⅝-inch dowel rods, wood or steel

Handsaw

Craft paint and small brush

Brass gooseneck brackets and hanging hardware

Epoxy glue

S hooks and leather cord, optional

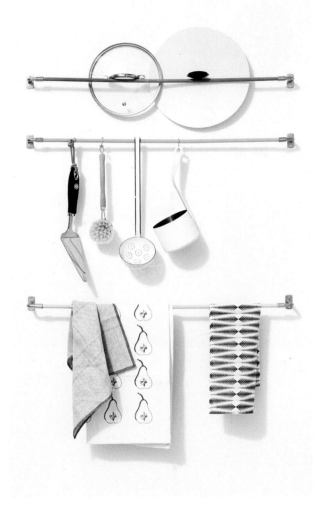

1. Depending on intended use, choose a hardwood or steel dowel rod (steel is better for heavier objects).

2. Cut dowel rod to desired length with a saw (the ones shown are 24 inches).

3. Paint rod desired color with craft paint; let dry.

4. Screw one gooseneck bracket into place on wall (use plastic wall anchors, if needed). Add a little glue to each end of dowel rod; place rod into first bracket, then into second. Secure with glue.

5. Screw second bracket to wall. Hang items on rods, using S hooks (and leather loops, if desired) for utensils.

Raised Pet Feeder

An elevated ledge makes eating more comfortable for your dog—and it looks better too. Using a jigsaw, cut a stair tread to 28 inches; trace inverted bowls onto tread and saw holes ⁷⁄₁₆ inch smaller than circles. Sand edges. Paint tread and wood brackets. Mount with anchors and screws at a height that equals your dog's "armpits." Place filled bowls in designated spots for chow time.

Cork Bulletin Board

Modular 12-inch cork tiles let you design a custom pinboard to fit any space—you can cut them if they don't align perfectly. Use it to hold a rotating selection of kids' artwork, photos, and other ephemera intermingled with more functional items like calendars and claim tickets that might otherwise get lost in the shuffle. The squares, available at office-supply stores, come with mounting tape, for hole-free installation.

Bathroom

Designated-Color Supplies

When multiple kids share the same bathroom, it's all too common for their towels and toothbrushes to get mixed up. Help them keep track of it all by letting each kid pick a favorite hue and providing them with coordinating supplies. Place small items directly above the peg or hook where each towel is hung.

Basket Storage

Pedestal sinks are stately, sure, but they're also short on storage. For a streamlined fix, stash essentials in baskets hung from a peg rail or individual hooks (designate some hooks for towels too, and even a mirror). For hanging straps, thread a leather cord through the weave and knot ends on inside to secure.

Toiletry Two-in-One

For a space-saving unit that's also stylish, upcycle a pair of kitchen basics to house two of your most essential bathroom supplies. All you need is a small glass that will nestle inside a widemouthed decanter (experiment to find the right match). Then store cotton balls in the jar below and cotton swabs in the glass above.

Instant Bathtub Caddy

Here's the simplest solution to the clawfoot tub's biggest design flaw—no storage spot. Visit a lumberyard or home-supply store and have a board (this one is about 1 inch thick and 8 inches wide) cut just a few inches longer than the width of the tub. Lay it in place and outfit it with your oils and soaps, some fragrant flowers, that book you're longing to get lost in—everything you need for a luxurious soak. Since it's not attached, it's no problem to relocate the board when not in use.

Dressing Area

Carryall Kits

Most totes are roomy but lack sufficient inner compartments, leaving you rummaging for your essentials. That's where clear-sided pouches are a boon: Use them to create mini kits, designating one for each category of items—cosmetics, work IDs and parking or transit passes, customer loyalty cards (better yet, keep those on a phone app), keys, and so on. This system also enables you to swap out your bag on a whim.

**CLASSIC
GOOD THING**

Clothing
Fix-It Kit

Clear business-card-holder sleeves from an office-supply store are just right for keeping all those little mending provisions handy (an idea that appeared in *Martha Stewart Living,* March 2007). Label each spare button or bit of thread before sliding it into one of the slots.

Pull-Out Shelf

In a closet, a work surface—for folding knitwear before putting it on the shelf, for instance—is a must. If yours doesn't have one, try this simple solution: Attach a pull-out plywood shelf with under-mount guides (from a hardware store) that can slide back when not in use. Then, for the neatest folds, use a small (about 8-by-10-inch) plastic cutting board as a guide.

Vanity Bench

With its flip-up seat, a piano bench repurposed for the vanity will stow all your beauty essentials. Paint, add a cushion (Velcro fabric-covered foam to the seat), and line the interior with paper and clear trays.

4

WAYS TO

ORGANIZE JEWELRY

Old-fashioned jewelry boxes don't compare to these clever solutions, created simply by repurposing items with inherent storage (spindles on a spool rack, nooks in an artist's tray) or upcycling a collection of attractive dishes. They'll keep your bangles in good order—and even double as décor.

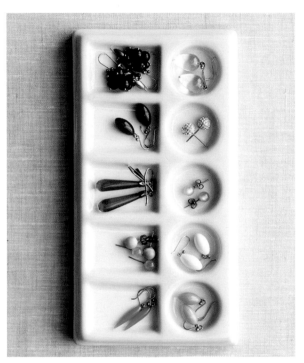

ON A SPOOL RACK

Meant for organizing sewing thread, these wooden holders have pegs that are perfect for keeping all your baubles neat and tidy. Look for vintage racks at flea markets and antique stores; mount one to a wall or, if it has legs, rest it on your vanity.

IN A PAINT PALETTE

A ceramic artist's tray as pretty and practical as this one can serve more than its intended purpose (i.e., holding paint). Try one out as a canvas for a collection of earrings—arranged by color, of course. It's flat, so you can tuck it into a drawer for safekeeping.

AMONG LITTLE DISHES

Employ a mismatched set of porcelain bowls and other dishes as dresser-drawer "inserts." Sort jewelry (along with hair accessories and cosmetics) into the vessels. Line drawer with adhesive wallpaper or coat it with paint for a touch more glamour.

ATOP CAKESTANDS

Footed dishes of varying heights and designs elevate a vanity to be chic, not shabby. Pair flea-market finds, upturning teacups and bowls for the bases and attaching plates, saucers, even fluted baking dishes with hot glue, on low setting; let set before using.

Office/Craft Space

Short-Order Track

Keeping your workstation in check will be a cinch with this inexpensive rail (or ticket holder)—it's what restaurants use to stay on top of a steady stream of orders. (Look for them online or at restaurant-supply stores.) Mount one above your desk, then load it up with all your ephemera. Marbles inside the track hold papers securely underneath. A groove on top keeps photos and postcards in place.

Color-Blocked Workspace >

Beat desktop clutter while keeping necessities within reach: Arrange painted pegboards (organizing workhorses), magnetic sheet metal panels, and chalkboard in an orderly grid.

THE DETAILS

- Vary the orientation of the pegboards and metal to fit your space.

- Spray-paint the hardware gold to unify (and elevate).

- Create zones on the pegboards—such as a wrapping station vs. craft supplies.

- Stow thumbtacks and other tiny objects in magnetic lidded jars.

- Bonus: For a generous work surface, rest a hollow-core door across two sawhorses, all painted with scuff-resistant high-gloss paint. Screw a yardstick to the desk if you measure on repeat.

Desk Organizer

The easiest mood board ever: Spray-paint a metal garden lattice, let it dry, and prop it up over your workspace or hang it on the wall. Use binder clips to hold inspirational items.

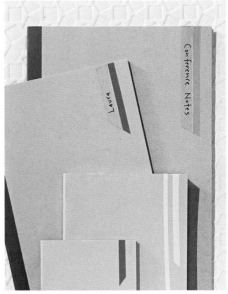

Washi-Tape Labels

Japanese washi tape is not just for kids' crafts. It can also be fun and functional in your workspace. Use it to create labels in different hues for an at-a-glance organizing system for notebooks or file folders. You can write on the labels, or just choose a different color for each family member and/or record-keeping category, such as household bills, school and medical records, or recipes.

Stenciled Holders

Magazine file boxes offer a neat way to keep periodicals and other printed material from piling up—but it's easy to lose track of what you've got in there. Rather than a boring label, try stenciling each box with a modern number or letter form, to identify the contents with style.

Scissor Saver

Your scissors will stay sharper longer when they're used exclusively for either fabric or paper, not both. So that you and others will know which is which, mark each pair with a looped piece of washi tape (or ribbon)—assign a color for each (such as blue for fabric, orange for paper), or label tape with a marker to be on the safe side.

Ribbon-Scrap Keeper

In the interest of not wasting a single scrap, wind all your ribbon odds and ends around a small rectangular piece of (upcycled) cardboard. Group them by color, as here, or material (velvet vs. grosgrain, for example), and secure each one with a ball pin. Store the pieces upright in a box or bin, for easy access.

Wrapping Station

Holidays aside, kraft paper is an all-purpose gift wrap that suits any occasion, even no occasion at all! Outfit a craft hutch or storage unit with cut-to-size 1-inch-diameter wooden dowels to make the heavy rolls more manageable. Use slimmer dowels to hold spools of string and twine. Then just unroll what you need.

Kids

Double-Duty Dresser

The sides of furniture pieces are usually wasted opportunities for expanding storage—especially in a kid's room. Affixing slim-profile wooden crates like these can even encourage little ones to put away their stuff.

1. First, paint the crates to match the dresser with two or three coats of paint—this is also a good time to give a tired piece new life with a fresh color.

2. Then remove the drawers and drill holes from the inside that line up with the four corners of each crate's side. Secure the crates with nuts and bolts.

3. Be sure to position crates the same on either side for balanced weight—especially if the piece is tippable. And don't forget to anchor the dresser to the wall using plastic anchors and screws.

Library Book Box

Borrowing books from a local library is a smart way to develop active readers. To make sure the titles are returned on time, mount a wooden bin by the door and let your literary lions decorate the front (paint it first if you like) and even tuck in a favorite toy or two.

Dollhouse Cabinet >

Besides being cute enough to keep in the kitchen, this miniature dwelling models homekeeping 101—and offers bonus storage for all your little ones' stuff. Start with a basic cabinet that comes with doors. Cut foam board to size for the walls; attach decorative paper with spray mount. Add room-appropriate furnishings. Tuck bins on the bottom floor to store life-size toys and books.

Stackable Comfort

Take a cue from traditional Japanese design and strew tatami mats and cushions throughout the house—perfect for impromptu reading, playing, even sleeping (with a futon mattress on top). The woven pieces wipe clean, stack easily, and come in kid and grown-up sizes, for family game night.

Locker Storage

Assign old-school lockers the job of containing kids' stuff in a garage or mudroom. For the sports-gear unit below, cut (painted) pegboard to interior wall dimensions, minus ⅛-inch on all sides; paint on item silhouettes so kids know what goes where. Screw to a frame made with ¾-inch molding secured to back of locker (this leaves space behind pegboard so S hooks can be attached). Stick magnetic hooks to door and inside walls; use a laundry bag to hold a gaggle of balls.

Tip

Designate a locker for each family member (so Mom has a place to stash her yoga mat and bicycle helmet, for example) or activity. You can even relegate an entire locker just for everyone's sneakers, hanging them in shoe bags that are suspended from a dowel slid through the pre-drilled holes.

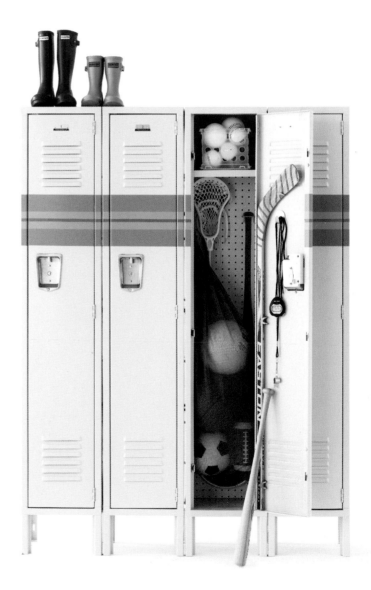

4

WAYS TO

INSPIRE KIDS' CREATIVITY

The goal: encouraging your little one's creativity, day in and day out. The reality: an abundance of hard-to-store supplies and a prolific output. Turn to the ideas below for solutions that tick all these boxes—and ensure you and your budding artist can bask in the moment.

TRAVEL CRAFT KIT

Banish boredom en route to or at your destination with a canvas tool bag (from a hardware store) packed with maker must-haves. The side pouches are just right for holding scissors, hole punches, and rulers. Carry washable paint or knickknacks in plastic divided containers; stow markers and glue sticks in their own bin. Once back home, just fold the bag away for storage.

POP-UP ART STUDIO

In many homes, the refrigerator door is the default display case for children's handiwork. Why not also use it as a makeshift (and easy-to-clean) easel? After all, even if you have a designated craft room, kids want to be where you are. Repurpose magnetic tiles to hold drawing paper in place (their colors and shapes can inspire the art) and magnetic tool bins to house brushes and (non-permanent!) paint or markers.

ART HOUSE

Give kids an indoor hideaway they can personalize. Build a simple tent frame with four 1-by-2-by-48-inch wood moldings; use a ¾-inch spade bit to drill holes, 6 inches from one end of each. Align pairs at holes; insert a 48-by-¾-inch wooden dowel into both. Splay legs. Hem plain canvas to 44 by 83½ inches. Drape over dowel; sew ribbon to corners and tie to feet. Protect floor before kids paint on their design.

PORTABLE WORKSTATION

You never know when or where a kid will be inspired to create, so turn a tiered utility cart into a mobile studio. The bottom shelf holds a deli paper cutter (equipped with a safeguard) for unspooling drawing paper; sort other supplies into wipeable enamelware containers, including a grab-and-go caddy on top. Trays double as paint palettes and crafting surfaces (with sides!) to keep beads and other items from getting lost.

Garden/Outdoor Spaces

Gardening Hutch

Along with an arsenal of tools, growing a beautiful garden requires copious planning and preparation. Why not spend a pre-season weekend creating a planting command center? Rather than starting from scratch, tweak an existing craft hutch—look for one with chalkboard (for to-do lists) and corkboard inside the doors. Pin binder clips to the corkboard to hold seed packets. Add hooks to the cabinet back for hanging tools. Corral clay pots, watering cans, and gardening books on built-in shelves (and on top); tuck catalogs into drawers.

Bike-Basket Repository

No bike? No problem. You can still use that charming cycling accessory you've been hanging on to—it's just the thing to hold gloves, twine, and small gardening tools. You might repurpose a basket that's missing the handlebar strap, or simply remove a still-intact strap from a new one. Hang the bin by its holes on a peg rail or other wall hooks.

Twig Trellis

Fallen (or pruned) branches are in ample supply come spring. Use them in a makeshift trellis for a rustic touch in the garden. Gather four like-size branches; wrap them about 6 inches from the tops with twine. Set support in soil around sweetpea, tomato, or cucumber seedlings—they'll climb as they grow.

Winter Supply Station

Lidded galvanized buckets and feed-bucket holders (sold at farm-supply shops or home-supply stores) are designed to withstand the elements. They are also handsome enough to be on view—so you can display the pails in a handy spot, for easy replenishing of bird feeder seed or deicing the driveway (add a scoop to each). When done, just slip the buckets into the holder rings that are mounted to an exterior wall (hardware is included). Come spring, swap in garden tools and outside toys for kids or pets.

CLASSIC GOOD THING

Trellis Organizer

Pick up a spare trellis—with its ready-made grid—from the garden center to contain a growing collection of supplies, as shown in *Martha Stewart Living*, March 2003. Mount it horizontally inside a shed or garage: At the top of every other vertical strip, drill a pilot hole with a ⅛-inch bit, then insert a 1¼-inch No. 10 screw to attach the trellis to the wall. Suspend tools from S hooks and use binder clips for seed packets or other items that don't have convenient holes for hanging.

Portable Plant Stand

Those wooden scooters from your grade-school gym class? Their non-marking rubber casters and full-perimeter bumpers also make them ideal (back-saving) stands for heavy potted trees. Just keep the plant on the scooter (you can hide it with burlap or embrace the utilitarian look) and then roll it whenever you need to vacuum or the plant needs a new home.

Twig Tags

Whittle stray branches (about ½ inch in diameter) to create fitting plant markers. Maple is easily worked but sturdy. With a vegetable peeler, strip a couple of inches from one end; use a permanent marker to jot plant name on the flat surface.

Summer Storage

Banish drippy, sandy gear from your house by creating a landing spot outside. Painted to match your home's exterior siding, a sturdy peg rail will keep all those seasonal items organized and off the ground. Mount the rail to wall studs with 2-inch screws, then hang beach chairs, tote bags, and other gear to dry between uses.

Make-Ahead
Marvels,
PAGE 151

4

Cooking

Of all the chapters in this book, this one might just
make the biggest difference in your daily life. After all, you can
use these tips three meals a day, seven days a week.
Being a canny home cook boils down to making the most of what
you have. Start with no-waste ideas for your ingredients
and test-kitchen tricks to make your tools and equipment even more
useful. Efficiency also counts, and hints like the best
way to strip kale, chop onions, and cook one-pan suppers will
save you time. Make-aheads are here too, so you can put
weeknight meals on the table with ease.

Kitchen Wisdom

Freezing Summer Fruit

The season is fleeting, but you can savor the just-picked flavor of fruits and vegetables for months to come.

TOMATOES: Freezing peeled tomatoes makes for simple work later: Score a small X on bottom of each; drop into boiling water until skins split. Plunge into an ice-water bath, then peel and freeze in a resealable freezer bag.

BERRIES AND CHERRIES: These will freeze with their flavor and texture intact. Hull or pit fruit, freeze in a single layer on a baking sheet until firm, then pop into resealable bags.

STONE FRUIT: Once peaches, plums, apricots, and nectarines are fragrant but still firm, pit, slice, and toss with a crushed vitamin C tablet for every pound of fruit, to prevent browning, then freeze as you would berries.

Repurposed Tools for Prepping Fruit

1. EGG SLICER: This device also sections strawberries into thin, uniform slivers. Simply hull fruit, place inside opening, and press.

2. CONTAINER LIDS: Layered singly between two rimmed lids, a dozen cherry tomatoes can be halved in one shot with a very sharp knife.

3. PEELER: Use the pointy tip to scoop out seeds from a stemmed small chile, like a jalapeño or serrano.

1

2

3

Eco-Friendly Produce Bags

Skip the plastic and hoist nautical-inspired cotton-mesh bags like these—designed for fishermen to haul their catch (and keep it fresh)—to use as stylish market totes and practical storage in one. Simply sort potatoes, onions, garlic, and other "keeper" vegetables into different bags, then hang them from a peg rail or hooks in the kitchen. The mesh will let air circulate, delaying any sprouting or softening.

Versatile Potato Ricer

Sure, it makes the lightest, finest mashed potatoes—reason enough to keep one of these tools in your arsenal. But this old-school gadget has modern-day tricks up its sleeve too. Use it to purée fruit (including cranberries and tomatoes) when making jams and sauces; squeeze excess water from cooked spinach and other greens; mince lots of garlic or fresh ginger at once; squeeze quartered citrus fruit; and "chop" hard-cooked eggs, such as for mimosa.

Herb Sachet

Rather than buying bunches of different herbs to flavor stocks, soups, braises, and roasts, buy a pre-assembled "poultry" assortment—it'll save you money and angst (no spoiled remains). These bundles often contain rosemary, thyme, sage, and savory or chervil, and can be used interchangeably with those called for in a specific recipe.

Storing Basil

Tender basil fades fast in the refrigerator. If you want it to last, keep it in a makeshift "greenhouse" instead. Rest a bunch in a glass with just the stems in water (trim them first as you would cut flowers) and the leaves above the rim. Then loosely place a clear produce bag over the top, with air inside, using a rubber band or twine to secure. The herbs will last for at least a week as long as you change the water every day or so.

4 Multi-Use Graters

Are these basic tools underutilized in your kitchen? Here are some pretty sharp ways to put them to work.

1. BOX GRATER: Each side has extra applications: Use the tiniest holes to break up hardened brown sugar; medium to make chocolate curls or zucchini "noodles"; and big to "chop" hard-cooked eggs (plus see page 127). The slots slice vegetables paper thin.

2. GINGER GRATER: Besides fresh ginger, this (often ceramic) tool makes fast work of finely mincing garlic cloves and fresh wasabi, turmeric, and horseradish.

3. RASP GRATER: It makes the fluffiest citrus zest and can quickly mill chocolate, whole spices such as nutmeg, and garlic too.

4. ROTARY GRATER: Meant for a block of hard cheese, it's also useful for pulverizing nuts and chocolate into fine powder, as you might when garnishing a dessert.

Tip

When using a rasp model, hold it upside down on whatever you are grating; your yield will pile on top for easy measuring and cleanup.

RECIPE PREREQUISITE

The classic French mise en place ("set in place") will save you time: Measure and cut ingredients for a recipe before you begin and keep them in small dishes, near the stove or your workspace. You'll never discover in the middle of cooking that you're short on something again.

Stripping Kale

You can use your hands to quickly strip the tender leaves from the tough stalks (a must when using kale in salads or cooking), or better yet, employ a large metal spoon with drain holes: Slip a stem through one of the holes, pull, et voilà!

Cutting Onions

There's more than one way to slice an onion, and doing it properly—as indicated in a recipe—helps ensure the dish comes out right. Here's a glossary of the most common sizes and cuts for all types of onions. Note that "finely chopped," or diced, is what's usually called for when an onion is part of the flavor-building base for sauces and soups.

1. MINCED: smaller than ⅛ inch

2. FINELY CHOPPED: smaller than ¼ inch

3. COARSELY CHOPPED: slightly larger than ¼ inch

4. SLICED: about ¼ inch thick

Prepping Garlic

When you need to peel a whole head, try this fun trick: Put it in a bowl (first whack it with the side of a chef's knife for a jump start), hold a matching bowl on top with rims touching, and firmly shake for 20 seconds or so. The cloves will be separated and peeled! To peel one or two cloves, smash them with the side of a chef's knife—they'll pop right out. For no-stick mincing, sprinkle peeled cloves with a pinch of coarse salt and a drop of olive oil before you begin. When making garlic paste (such as for dips and marinades), drag the side of the knife across minced garlic several times.

Washing Greens >

Giving lettuces and other leafy greens an ice bath will crisp them up—especially if they are looking a little tired from being in the refrigerator for a few days. Throw prepped greens into a bowl of ice water in batches; swish them around to release any dirt. After removing the washed greens from the bath, spin them dry. Do this no more than a couple of hours before serving.

Draining Zucchini

For loaf cakes or fritters, grated zucchini must be "squeezed of excess moisture." Line a colander with a clean kitchen towel and grate the squash into it; lift and twist towel, forcing out the juice.

Peeling Ginger

The best tool for peeling fresh ginger? A regular metal spoon, as shown below (*Martha Stewart Living*, August 2005). Unlike a paring knife, this utensil scrapes off only the thin skin so none of the root is wasted. Holding the knob with one hand, work the spoon, concave side facing you, over the ginger in short motions, reaching into the crevices. Refrigerate unused portion in a resealable plastic bag with the air pressed out.

CLASSIC GOOD THING

Sautéing Greens

Garlic is often used to impart depth to Swiss chard (shown here from the September 2001 issue of *Martha Stewart Living*) and other greens, such as kale and spinach. But with minced or chopped garlic, you risk overpowering—rather than enhancing—the final dish. Not to mention, it can quickly burn and turn unpleasantly bitter. For a subtler flavor boost, spear a large peeled clove with a fork and use it to stir the greens as you cook. You can even save the same clove to use again by wrapping it in plastic wrap and refrigerating up to two days in a small airtight container or resealable plastic bag (the double layer will help keep the odors from emanating).

Trimming Asparagus

Trimming off just the woody end of asparagus is a snap—literally. Hold each spear and then gently break it near the base; it should separate cleanly, leaving you with only the most tender part. To revive wilted asparagus, stand the trimmed spears in a glass of ice water for about an hour, until plump.

Cleaning Mushrooms >

Cleaning mushrooms with a vegetable brush is slow work (and doesn't always remove all the grit). Try this shortcut: Float button or cremini mushrooms in a bowl of cool water (not shiitake, they will get soggy), gently agitating them with your hands to release stubborn dirt. Drain on a towel; prep and cook right away.

ground cinnamon

ground ginger

cumin seeds

red pepper flakes

whole
cloves

sweet paprika

whole nutmeg

whole allspice

cayenne pepper

Must-Have Spices

Looking to streamline your spice drawer? It doesn't make sense to overstock—spices don't come cheap and they can lose their potency before you use them up. Begin with these nine essentials, adding others according to your repertoire. Buy whole spices when possible and grind as needed; they last longer than ground (a year vs. six months). Unsure that a ground spice is still good? Give it a sniff—it should smell fresh and potent, not dull. Store all spices in a cool, dark, dry spot.

Pantry Powerhouses

Some well-chosen bottles, jars, and tubes can bring serious impact to your cooking. These are just some test-kitchen favorites to try.

SAMBAL OELEK: For fiery heat, add a spoonful of this Asian chili sauce at the end of cooking eggs, vegetables, and stir-fries, or in a marinade for tofu or shrimp.

ANCHOVY PASTE: Easier than fishing out fillets from a tin, the paste adds umami to marinades, dressings, sauces, pasta dishes, and vegetable sautés.

TOMATO PASTE: A little goes a long way to boost sauces and stews. Look for the double-concentrated variety.

SHERRY VINEGAR: Mellower than regular wine vinegar, less sweet than balsamic, sherry vinegar is a nuanced, pleasing pick for vinaigrettes and glazes.

GOMASIO (JAPANESE SESAME SALT): Sprinkle on steamed vegetables, popcorn, broiled fish, and salads for a nutty kick.

SALT-PACKED CAPERS: Less salty (when rinsed) than those in vinegar, these tiny pickled buds add Mediterranean flair to salad dressings, fish and chicken sauces (think piccata), and pasta dishes.

Lemon Zest Booster

Grated lemon zest adds brightness to many savory dishes. When lightly fried, until crisp and caramelized, the zest offers an even bigger boost. Remove the yellow rind of two lemons with a vegetable peeler; slice peels into thin matchsticks. Cook zest in ¼ inch of olive oil over medium-high heat for just a few seconds. Strain oil before serving, or use oil and zest together in a marinade or dressing, or as a last-minute garnish for fish or vegetables.

Salad Upgrades

Skip the limp, prewashed lettuces from the supermarket and make your own tasty, crunchy medley. For the classic tri-color mix, combine a head each of romaine, radicchio, and endive. Or try baby arugula, spinach, and kale. You can also rev up your salads with fresh herbs. Leafy varieties with tender stems, like chervil and cilantro, can be tossed in by the sprig.

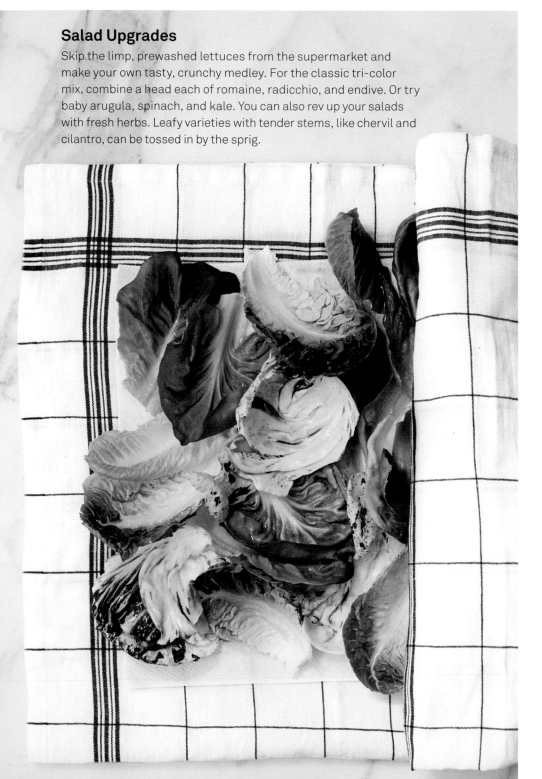

HERE ARE A FEW
PAIRINGS TO TRY:

Chervil + **Butter Lettuce**

Italian Parsley + **Leaf Lettuce**

Cilantro + **Romaine**

Tarragon + **Frisée**

Grated Butter

No time to wait for butter to reach room temperature? Grate the still-cold butter on the large holes of a box grater onto a piece of parchment. The little pieces will soften faster than a solid stick. Grating also makes quick work of cutting cold butter into biscuit and pie doughs, without overmixing.

Smoother Blending

If you've ever had to contend with a blender jam when whizzing up your morning smoothie, you'll appreciate this simple solution: Combine the ingredients in the right order so the frozen chunks won't get stuck in the blades. Start by adding the yogurt, or a liquid such as juice or milk, to the blender jar. Next, put in smaller ingredients, like diced mango or whole blueberries and raspberries, and top off with larger ones, such as sliced bananas, hulled strawberries, and ice cubes (if using). For the smoothest, stall-free blend, use a mix of frozen and fresh fruit rather than all frozen.

No-Sink Berries

For plump berries in every bite, toss them with a teaspoon of flour from the recipe before mixing them into your muffin batter. The flour coating will help absorb the fruit's juices during baking, so they'll stay aloft rather than sinking to the bottom.

Flakier Biscuits

Martha's rule of thumb when making biscuits from scratch is to "work cold, bake hot." The following tips will help you heed this advice:

- Always start with well-chilled butter when mixing, and work quickly to keep it from melting. If the butter begins to soften, freeze the mixture for about 10 minutes.

- Don't overmix or overwork the dough, which can produce tough biscuits. The butter should remain in small pieces (grated butter cuts in quickly; see page 127).

- Bake the biscuits in a hot oven—400°F or higher. This ensures that the bits of butter melt quickly, creating the steam that lifts the dough and adds height to the flaky layers.

Tip

Never lose track of your dry ingredients again: Rest a fine-mesh sieve over your mixing bowl. Place the most plentiful ingredient (usually flour) in first. Add remaining ingredients in visible mounds. Then sift everything at once.

Chopstick Uses

Not just for eating: Use a sturdy pair of chopsticks to level dry ingredients, marble batters and frostings, imprint cookie doughs, and secure cake layers (in place of dowels). They're also good for pitting cherries, scrambling eggs, fluffing rice, and flipping delicate items (like dumplings) or even digging out olives and capers from a jar.

Better Brewing

If your usual modus operandi is to pour boiling water over a tea bag and drink, you've been missing out on your tea's full potential. Try this method:

1. Heat a kettle of water, ideally filtered; see right for temperature recommendations.

2. Pour ½ cup of the hot water into a 10-to-12-ounce teapot, and swirl it around to warm pot up, about 5 seconds; discard water.

3. Spoon 4 grams tea leaves (1 to 3 rounded tablespoons, depending on density of leaves) directly into teapot or into a basket strainer (or metal ball) inside pot.

4. Fill teapot with the heated water and let steep (see right for brewing times).

5. When tea is ready, decant it or remove basket strainer (or ball) to stop the steeping.

HEAT AND STEEP

Recommended temperatures and times for 12 ounces of water and 4 grams of tea.

BLACK: 205°F (just off a boil); 3 minutes

GREEN: 180°F (when you see steam); 2 minutes

TISANE: 205°F (just off a boil); 3 to 4 minutes

WHITE: 180°F (when you see steam); 2 minutes

PU-ERH: 205°F (just off a boil); 3 minutes

OOLONG: 190°F to 205°F (just off a boil); 2 minutes

Foolproof Scrambled Eggs

Even for this supremely simple mainstay, following the right method ensures best results. Start by whisking three eggs until whites and yolks are combined (skip the milk!); season with salt and pepper. Then cook as follows to create soft, pillowy curds:

1. Melt 1 tablespoon butter in an 8-inch nonstick skillet over low heat; add eggs.

2. Pull eggs to center of pan with a heatproof spatula, allowing liquid part to run to edge. (Don't overstir—that creates tiny curds.)

3. Remove eggs as soon as they look set but are still slightly wet; they'll continue to firm up a bit off the heat.

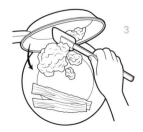

Crisp Waffles

Patience and practice are on your side. First, preheat your waffle iron, and start with room-temperature ingredients—cold batters are prone to being undercooked. Next, resist the urge to peek under the lid until each waffle is fully cooked. It's ready when the steam stops billowing out. Remove waffle, then do this test-kitchen trick: Gently toss it back and forth between your hands several times, to allow more steam to escape before the waffle hits the plate (avoiding a soggy underside).

The Perfect Fluff and Fold ⟩

Textbook omelet, demystified: Whisk a splash of water into three room-temp eggs—it will create steam when the eggs hit the hot, buttered pan, giving them a little lift. Don't overwhisk; stop when eggs drip smoothly from fork tines. Cook quickly, until just set, toss in some cheese and fresh herbs, then serve the omelet like a pro: Slide it halfway onto plate, then use pan to fold it over onto itself.

Sheet-Pan Suppers

Rimmed baking sheets are ideal for making weeknight meals with minimal fuss and cleanup. A standard 13-by-18-inch aluminum "half sheet" is roomy enough and gets piping hot fast, while the low rim speeds up browning.

1. BUILD A SOLID BASE: Roots and tubers (beets, parsnips, carrots, potatoes), crucifers (broccoli, cauliflower, brussels sprouts, cabbage), winter squashes, and sturdy greens (kale, chard, collards) are all tailor-made for this technique, which will leave them tender and caramelized. Cut vegetables into uniform pieces for even cooking.

2. LAYER IN PROTEIN: Fish fillets, chicken breasts and thighs, pork chops, and sausages are your best bets. Chickpeas and other beans or sliced tofu (the firm or extra-firm variety works best) are vegetarian options.

3. FINISH WITH TOPPINGS: Fresh herbs, capers or olives, citrus zest and juice, grated cheese, seasoned breadcrumbs, pesto, and/or a drizzle of olive oil and a sprinkle of flaky sea salt will all boost flavor and eye appeal.

Tip

Roast denser vegetables like sweet potatoes until tender before adding quicker-cooking items like the spinach and sea bass fillets in this one-pan wonder (a parsley-caper-vinegar "salsa" is drizzled on at the end).

Tortilla Tactics

All you need is a muffin tin or some crumbled-up foil to bake tacos and tortilla cups at home—and without the mess of deep frying. They'll keep for days, so you can fill the crispy, crunchy vessels with your favorite toppings for a kid-friendly lunch or dinner in a flash.

1. BAKED TACO SHELLS: Lightly brush six (6-inch) corn tortillas on both sides with vegetable oil. Flip a standard muffin pan upside down; nestle tortillas in the space between the muffin cups to form shell shapes. Bake in a 375°F oven until crisp, 12 to 15 minutes. Let cool slightly in pan.

2. BAKED TACO BOWLS: Lightly brush four (8-inch) flour tortillas on both sides with vegetable oil. Drape over balls of aluminum foil (about the size of tennis balls). Bake directly on oven rack at 375°F until crisp, about 15 minutes. Let cool. (Flatten the foil to reuse it.)

MAKE AHEAD
Store the baked shells or bowls in an airtight container at room temperature for up to 3 days.

Fresh-Looking Guacamole

Despite what you may think, you can make guacamole a few hours or even a day ahead without sacrificing its vibrant color. Pack it in an airtight container and cover with plastic wrap, pressing it directly on the surface of the dip (not just over the container). This way you're limiting the exposure to air—and preventing it from turning brown.

Multi-Use Tongs

Flipping steaks on the grill is just the beginning. Use these inexpensive pinchers to juice citrus halves—such as when making lemonade, as shown here—or to toss a salad, twirl pasta, cook stir-fries, turn food in a hot oven, and fish out items (such as corn cobs) from boiling water.

Tip Your cast-iron skillet should be re-seasoned regularly to remain nonstick and rust-free: After cleaning it (see page 52), slick the inside surface with canola oil, then heat in a 350°F oven for 1 hour.

Three Indispensable Pans

Forget about buying a whole set—these three workhorses will cover all your cooking needs.

1. HEAVY METAL: Sturdy cast iron stands up to high heat, for pan-frying, roasting, grilling, and baking cakes and crisps. Avoid acidic items like citrus, vinegar, soy, and tomato sauces; these might make your food take on a metallic flavor.

2. SQUEAKY CLEAN: Durable nonstick, with a titanium-reinforced ceramic coating, is dishwasher- and oven-safe (below 400°F). Use it for eggs, braises, and baked lasagna (or other clingy cheese dishes).

3. HEAT CONDUCTOR: Lightweight stainless steel gets hot fast—perfect for quick stir-fries, one-pot dishes, and steamed vegetables. Sticky foods can discolor the surface, but acidic ones are fair game.

Grilling Salmon

Salmon and other types of fish are delicious when grilled, but can stick to the hot grates. Rather than buying a special basket (yet another tool to clean and store), cook the fish, using indirect heat and a covered grill, on a bed of orange and lime slices. The fruit will impart flavor and become wonderfully caramelized, juicy, and fragrant—perfect to serve alongside. The same idea works for other types of fish and also boneless, skinless chicken breast halves. You can swap out the citrus too, for lemons, ruby grapefruit (sweeter than other types), and all manner of oranges (including blood oranges and Cara Cara).

Boning a Fillet

Don't let the thought of removing tiny pin bones from fish fillets keep you from cooking this superfood at home. It is a simple process—and worth the little bit of extra time. Your fishmonger may have already removed the bones for you; if not (or if they missed a few), use this method to find and extract them:

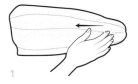

1. Drape fillet over an upside-down bowl, skin-side down. Lightly run your fingers along center of fillet, from narrow end to wider end, to feel for bones. Do the same along top and bottom thirds.

2. Gently wiggle and pull bones free using needle-nose pliers or fish tweezers. Pull in same direction they're sticking out to prevent tearing the fish. Wipe each bone from tips of tool on a paper towel before moving on to the next one.

Tip

If you plan to skin the fish, do so with a sharp, thin-bladed knife after deboning—the skin will help prevent tearing as you remove the bones.

Cooking a Whole Fish

Buying a whole fish can be more economical than fillets. It is also easier to handle one or two of these than multiple smaller pieces—and they're less prone to overcooking. A 2- to 3-pound fish will yield a 1-pound serving after cooking and removing the head and tail portions.

ROAST: A whole fish such as snapper, cod, or branzino (or other flaky whitefish) can be prepared the same way you would a chicken: Rub it with olive oil, sprinkle with salt and pepper, stuff the cavity with lemon and lime slices, dill and basil sprigs, and hot chiles (optional); roast at 450°F for 15 to 25 minutes depending on the size. Serve with more lime and lemon slices.

BAKE IN SALT: Encasing a whole fish in coarse salt (you'll need about 3 pounds) and baking it at 400°F for about 35 minutes will guarantee the flesh is the right degree of doneness, without making it overly saline (thanks to the skin). This also affords you a dramatic oven-to-table presentation if you wait to crack open the salt shell with the back of a spoon or a knife.

Mussel Prep

It's a wonder these mollusks aren't more appreciated as a seafood star. They're incredibly affordable, widely available, and quick-cooking. Plus, they're milder tasting and less briny than clams, and just as easy and foolproof to steam—they're ready when the shells open up. (See page 158 for one serving suggestion.)

1. Inspect each shell for cracks and openings, and discard any that have them (or that remain open when tapped).

2. Rinse mussels in cold water, scrubbing them with a scrub sponge or vegetable brush to remove sand and grit.

3. De-beard the mussels with your fingers: Simply grip the tough fibers that extend from the shell and pull them off.

Tip

Mussels can be refrigerated up to 2 days before cooking; store them in the mesh bag they came in (never plastic) or in a colander set over a dish, covered with a damp towel.

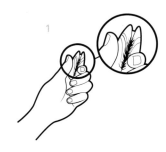

Poaching Fish

Of all the ways to prepare fatty fish like salmon and tuna, cold-poaching is the most foolproof, yielding silky flesh every time. It's also a great make-ahead. Slash fish (preferably skin-on; fat adds flavor) a few times to prevent curling. Combine with cold water to cover in a pot, add aromatics such as leeks, lemon slices, celery stalks, bay leaves, and whole peppercorns, then bring liquid to a gentle simmer (it should be barely moving); cook until fish falls apart when pierced with a fork, 5 to 10 minutes. Remove fish with a slotted spatula to serve warm, or allow it to cool in liquid and refrigerate together in an airtight container up to 2 days and serve cold or at room temperature.

Vegetable Kebabs

Skewers are an efficient way to grill smaller pieces that might otherwise fall through the grates. Vegetables cook at different rates, however, so create kebabs of vegetables with similar cooking times, like the combos shown. Cut everything into same-size pieces and grill them over direct medium heat, turning once halfway through, until tender and lightly charred in spots.

Rack-Free Roast Poultry

A rack is only one way to elevate a chicken or turkey to keep it from sitting in its drippings (which prevents the skin from crisping up). Here are a couple of edible, no-waste alternatives: Roast the bird atop a smattering of thickly sliced rustic bread, adding thyme sprigs and peeled garlic cloves (as here) for extra seasoning. The drippings will make the bread toasty, not soggy—perfect for serving with the meal. Or use quartered onions and carrots, which will lend aromatic flavor as they cook.

Chicken Update

Meet the newest grilling star for your summer barbecues: chicken halves. They cook more evenly than a whole bird, and even the breast meat emerges juicy, thanks to the fat from the legs (and skin). Most supermarkets sell the halves already packaged; if yours doesn't, ask at the meat counter. Then give the pieces a yogurt bath to help tenderize without turning them mushy, as in this tandoori-style entrée. Season yogurt with curry paste (store-bought or your own), then rub the mixture all over chicken, being sure to get under the skin. Refrigerate in a resealable plastic bag (press out extra air) at least 12 hours and up to 1 day, and bring to room temperature about 1 hour before grilling. Let stand 15 minutes before serving with cooling accompaniments, including sliced cucumbers, fresh mint, and chutneys.

Tip

When grilling chicken halves, start the pieces over moderate indirect heat to cook through, 40 to 50 minutes, turning periodically, then finish over direct fire to crisp up the skin (watch carefully, as the yogurt can scorch).

WAYS TO

USE FRESH HERBS

Many recipes call for just a sprig or two from a whole bunch of herbs, leaving the rest to linger in your refrigerator's bin. Put them to use! They'll add a flavor boost to practically every summer meal, so start with these suggestions (plus the one on page 153)—and swap in whatever you have on hand.

CILANTRO

Taco—make that Tostada—Tuesday wouldn't be the same without a shower of cilantro as a topping. Here, both the stems and leaves also lend flavor to a smoky salsa that's made by blistering tomatillos, white onion wedges, garlic cloves, and jalapeños in a dry cast-iron skillet and then cooling and blitzing in a blender with cilantro, broth, lime juice, and salt.

BASIL

Versatile basil goes beyond Italian flavors. Try scattering a handful over stir-fries at the end of cooking; the residual heat will bring out its taste and aroma. Here, shrimp, snap peas, shiitake mushrooms, lemongrass, and Thai chiles are all sizzled before being tossed with soaked glass noodles and a go-to sauce: 2 tablespoons each soy sauce, fish sauce, and fresh lime juice, plus ¼ cup water.

MINT

Mojitos? Check. Mint makes a sprightly twist on pesto too: Pulse ½ cup packed mint leaves in a food processor with ½ cup shelled raw pistachios, 2 ounces grated Pecorino Romano, a small garlic clove, 2 teaspoons grated lemon zest, and salt to taste. Stream in ½ cup extra-virgin olive oil until combined. Fold into pasta dishes—this one has asparagus and cherry tomatoes—and sprinkle more mint on top.

OREGANO

If you tend to reach for dried, fresh oregano will be a revelation. It works wonders in a vinaigrette: Whisk together ¼ cup white-wine vinegar, 2 teaspoons Dijon mustard, and ½ cup extra-virgin olive oil; stir in 3 tablespoons chopped oregano. Add to mixed olives and hot-off-the-grill fish (let stand 10 minutes). Heap on a platter with baby greens and grilled onions and potatoes. Or drizzle over your favorite Greek salad.

Time Savers

Sturdy Greens

Blanching bunches of hearty greens as soon as you bring them home will save on space in the refrigerator—and save you time when you're in a rush to prepare dinner later in the week. It will also help you avoid forgetting them in the vegetable bin. Strip leaves from stems (see page 119 for a neat tip). Save edible Swiss chard stems to enjoy along with the leaves. Blanch greens in boiling salted water, about 15 seconds for spinach and chard and 2 minutes for kale and collards; drain and squeeze out excess liquid in a kitchen towel. Spread on a rimmed baking sheet to cool, then refrigerate in an airtight container up to 4 days or freeze and use within 3 months.

Whole Grains

The best way to store a big batch of cooked grains? Freeze individual servings—or enough for a meal—in plastic bags for up to 6 months. When ready to use, thaw them on your microwave's defrost setting, or drop the sealed bag in boiling water. You can also simply break off frozen chunks and toss them into soups and stews. Brown rice, red quinoa, bulgur, millet, purple barley, rye, and sorghum (shown here, from top to bottom) are all candidates, and interchangeable in recipes.

Roasted Vegetables

Roast a week's worth of vegetables on a sheet pan for adding to pasta, egg dishes (a frittata or an omelet), and sandwiches—basically anywhere you want their caramelized taste and healthy boost. Cut them so they cook evenly: Denser vegetables, like potatoes and carrots, should be a little smaller than ones that contain more water, like zucchini (or cook them on separate pans, pulling quicker-cooking ones sooner). Roast tomato halves open-side-up so they don't lose their juices. Let cool before refrigerating in airtight containers.

Frozen Salmon

Forget what you may think about buying frozen fish—choose wisely and you can have a stock of this heart-healthy protein on hand. (Many seafood stores and fish departments sell previously frozen fish, so there's no reason to assume their supply is "fresher" than what's in your freezer.) Look for salmon that is rapidly chilled right after the catch, which locks in just-caught freshness. Similar to shrimp, salmon need not be thawed before cooking. Simply remove it from its packaging, rinse it under cool water to wash away the ice glaze, and pat dry before poaching, steaming, baking, or grilling until it is opaque and flakes with a fork.

Bread-Freeze-Bake Cutlets

Stockpile breaded cutlets in your freezer for speedy dinners—they'll be ready after a mere 15 minutes in a 350°F oven. The secret to their crispy coating is pretoasting the panko: Toss 4 cups crumbs with ¼ cup olive oil and coarse salt and bake, tossing twice, until golden brown, about 15 minutes. Let cool completely, and crush a few handfuls, to help them adhere to the meat. Then bread chicken breast cutlets, which have been sliced or pounded thin, or try swapping in thigh cutlets, which are less likely to dry out: First dredge in flour, tapping off excess; dip in beaten eggs and then coat in panko, pressing to adhere. Freeze on a baking sheet in a single layer for 2 hours. Then stack between parchment and freeze in resealable bags, for up to 1 month. Bake just what you need at a time.

All-Purpose Breakfast Batter

Here's a time-saving batter that lets you make multiple goods in one fell swoop. Whisk 2 cups all-purpose flour, ½ cup sugar, 1¼ teaspoons baking powder, ½ teaspoon baking soda, and ½ teaspoon coarse salt. Stir in 1¼ cups buttermilk, 2 large eggs, 6 tablespoons melted unsalted butter, and 1 teaspoon vanilla extract until a few small lumps remain. Fold in fruit and/or nuts as desired. Bake muffins at 375°F for about 20 minutes; cook waffles until crisp (4 to 5 minutes) in a greased hot iron; cook ¼-cup-portion pancakes on a greased griddle until golden brown, flipping once, 4 to 6 minutes.

Tip

Although batter won't keep, you can freeze cooked pancakes or waffles from your weekend batch, for a fast breakfast any day of the week. Once cooled, freeze them in a single layer on a baking sheet until firm, then transfer to resealable freezer bags and use within two months. To serve, just pop them in a toaster oven, straight from the freezer.

Bake-Ahead Bacon

Cooking bacon on the stove leaves you with all that splattered grease to clean up. Instead, cook off a whole package of bacon on a wire rack set in a foil- or parchment-lined rimmed baking sheet (which you can toss) in a 350°F oven for about 30 minutes. Let cool completely, stack on paper towels, and refrigerate, covered in plastic wrap, up to 4 days. Reheat servings on a foil-lined rimmed baking sheet in a 300°F oven, 10 to 12 minutes.

Make-and-Freeze Burritos

Big-batch, from-scratch burritos let you skip the packaged varieties (and their questionable additives) for easy weeknight dinners. Sauté some minced garlic and chili powder, then stir in canned or cooked pinto or black beans; spread the mixture on a tortilla, and layer on desired fillings—for example, cooked rice, shredded cheese, roast chicken, sautéed summer squash, and baby spinach. Fold (as illustrated) and freeze in zipper-top bags up to 3 months. Heat in a 350°F oven, wrapped in foil, for 25 minutes (or remove foil and heat in the microwave); crisp in a hot pan with a little oil.

Salad Dressing Formula

You don't need a recipe when you commit this ratio to memory: Mix 4 parts fat, like olive oil or coconut oil (or even buttermilk/yogurt/mayo); 2 parts acid, as in lemon juice or vinegar; and 1 part flavor enhancer, such as honey, Dijon mustard, or fresh herbs. Skip the whisk too: Just put it all in a jar and shake to combine.

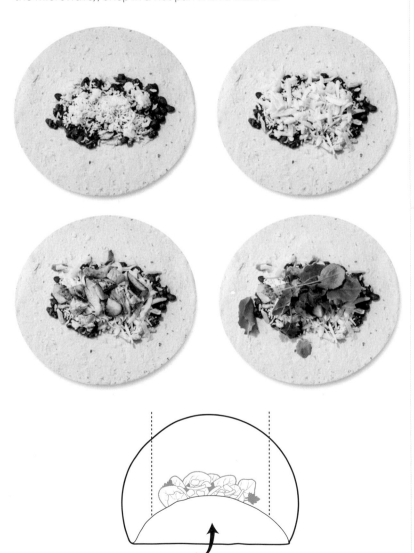

Quick-Preserve Lemons

Thin-skinned Meyer lemons are the secret to creating this Middle Eastern specialty on the quick. Slicing them finely (not into wedges) also helps. Toss 3 lemons with 1 tablespoon coarse salt and 3 tablespoons sugar; cover and let stand overnight, then refrigerate up to 2 weeks in a jar. Chop and add to vinaigrettes, marinades, and, of course, tagines.

Just-Add-Water Soups

Packing soup for lunch at the office can be tricky, what with the risk of leaks—and sodden produce and starches. The answer? In a glass storage container, layer quick-cooking ingredients like rice noodles, couscous, and extra-thinly sliced vegetables with condiments like miso, harissa, and chipotle (to flavor the broth). When you're ready to eat, fill container almost to top with water; seal and shake. Microwave (uncovered) for 2 minutes and enjoy, right from the container.

Make-Ahead Marvels

Some foods—soups full of seasonal vegetables like this one, braised meats, even sweets— taste better the second day. Use these categories to come up with your own standbys.

SOUPS AND STEWS: Left to meld overnight, the flavors of minestrone, chili, seafood chowder, gumbo, and curries come together as one.

PASTA SAUCES: Tomato-based marinara, Bolognese, and lamb or pork ragu will take on more nuance over time.

PIES AND CUSTARDS: Pie fillings, especially fruity ones, need time to set—a must for neat slices. Chilled custards (including ice cream) do too, becoming all the richer and creamier.

No-Waste Ideas

Extra Cabbage

It's always surprising how many cups of prepped cabbage a single head can yield, certainly more than the average recipe ever calls for. Use the rest to make a super-quick slaw: Toss about half a medium head of shredded cabbage with 2 tablespoons cider vinegar, ¼ cup extra-virgin olive oil, and a pinch of celery seed. Season with coarse salt. Cover and let stand 30 minutes to let the flavors meld and the cabbage soften before serving (or refrigerate, covered, up to 3 days).

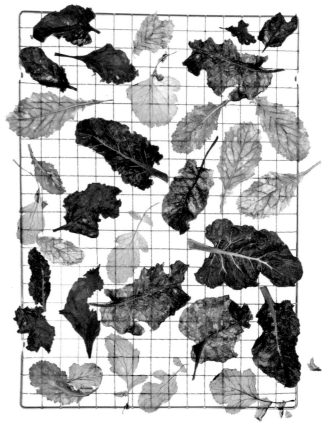

Root Greens

When trimming beets, turnips, and radishes, keep the leaves for making crunchy snacks, à la kale chips (Swiss chard, also shown here, works well too). Tear large leaves into 2-inch pieces; toss with olive oil to lightly coat. Season with sea salt. Bake in a single layer at 350°F until the leaves flatten, darken slightly, and become crisp, about 8 minutes. Let cool on a wire rack.

Infused Oil

Despite your best intentions, it can be hard
to use an entire bunch of herbs that you buy
for one recipe. Use the rest to infuse extra-
virgin olive oil with subtle flavor, then whisk
the oil into vinaigrettes and marinades or
drizzle over roasted or steamed vegetables
or fish. Combine 2 cups extra-virgin olive
oil with a handful of any fresh herb (or a
combination) in a large saucepan. Cook over
medium heat for 5 minutes (do not let boil).
Let cool, then strain and discard herbs.
Oil will keep in an airtight container in the
refrigerator for up to a month. Or simply
combine a few sprigs with oil in a jar, seal
and refrigerate 2 weeks, then remove the
herbs and keep the oil for another 2 weeks.

Broccoli Stalks

It's a wonder so many recipes call for only the florets—
the stalks are also delicious and add crunch to raw
slaws or this simple salad: Peel stalks just to remove
dark-green exterior, reserving any leaves; thinly slice.
Drizzle stalks and leaves with soy sauce and hot (spicy)
sesame oil; sprinkle with toasted sesame seeds.

Double-Duty Meatloaf ›

Besides being a delicious, family-pleasing dinner on its own, meatloaf is famously good as leftovers. It can easily be transformed into an entirely different meal for another busy weeknight. To give the usual glaze a new spin, spike ½ cup ketchup with 2 teaspoons each minced chipotle chile and adobo sauce. Serve the meatloaf with mashed sweet potatoes, watercress, and lime wedges, as here (or your own preferred sides). The next night, slather leftover slices (heated or cold!) with mayonnaise, layer with romaine and red onion on sesame-seed buns, and finish with more watercress and lime wedges. Take the same approach with meatballs, serving half with spaghetti and the remainder on DIY grinders.

Rendered Fat

Ever wondered what to do after you "skim the foam from the surface" when preparing chicken stock or soup? Don't discard it! This "schmaltz" is a classic ingredient in matzo balls and the secret to exceptional french fries; it also makes a rich, delicious spread for toast. (Let the strained broth chill overnight, and you can simply spoon off the fat that rises to the top.) Freeze in an airtight container for 6 months or longer.

Ditto the fat that is rendered off when cooking bacon, which will give a kick of smoky flavor to sweet and savory food. Save it and sub it for oil or butter in cornbread, scones, pancakes, and waffles; rub it over chicken before roasting; or use it for sautéing vegetables. Refrigerate in an airtight jar and use within 3 months.

Root-to-Stem Cooking

Seek out untrimmed root vegetables and you'll be rewarded with flavorful greens that will stretch your dollar—and expand your repertoire. Just be sure to remove the tops from the roots and store them separately, so they last longer. Wash and spin-dry before using in the following ways:

BEET AND TURNIP GREENS: Sauté with garlic or shallot in olive oil until wilted and satiny (similar to kale, Swiss chard, and spinach).

CELERY ROOT AND RADISH LEAVES: Add these raw to salads, or chop and mix into dips and spreads, as you would herbs.

HORSERADISH GREENS: Besides grating the root (rather than buying bottled), the peppery greens are a good stand-in for arugula in salads and sandwiches, or sautéed, similar to chard.

Carrot Tops

Carrots often come with an abundance of frilly tops intact—and they are every inch worth keeping for their earthy taste and vibrant color. These greens are particularly tasty in pesto. Simply replace half of the basil in your go-to recipe with the washed and dried tops, preferably swapping in walnuts or macadamia nuts for the traditional pine nuts, for complementary flavor. Toss it with roasted carrots for a vibrant side, or use any way you would traditional pesto.

Tomato Pulp

Next time you're "putting up" tomato sauce, reserve the typically tossed pulp for tomato water. The concentrated liquid—a secret of high-end chefs and mixologists—will give a sweet, summery boost to cocktails (think martinis and Bloody Marys) as well as salad dressings, chilled soups (like gazpacho), and risotto. To make it, add tomato pulp to a cheesecloth-lined fine-mesh sieve that's set over a bowl; refrigerate 8 to 24 hours. (For clear liquid, don't stir or press on the pulp.) Discard solids and refrigerate the liquid, covered, for up to 3 days, or freeze in an ice-cube tray (and then in a resealable plastic bag) to use all year long.

Leftover Wine

Once opened, most wine is only drinkable for one or two days at best. You can save it for cooking, however, by pouring the excess into an ice-cube tray, putting 1 to 2 tablespoons per section. Freeze until solid, then transfer the cubes to a resealable bag and use within 3 months. Toss them into soups, stews, braises, and other recipes as needed (thaw first if using in risotto).

Surplus Champagne

Sparkling wine loses its effervescence quickly, making it hard to keep opened bottles after a party. Don't pour it down the drain, however. Think of flat bubbly as a substitute for white wine, and you can see the potential for using it in all manner of dishes—steaming mussels (or clams), poaching fish or chicken, deglazing a pan (to stir up the flavorful browned bits, such as when making sauces), or cooking risotto. A dry variety (look for brut on the label) is best for savory dishes. Cover the bottle opening with plastic wrap and refrigerate for up to a month until ready to use.

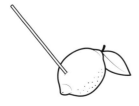

Squeeze-and-Save Lemons

Do this when you need just a splash of lemon juice (a common occurrence): Poke a wooden skewer halfway into the fruit near its nonstem end to create a small hole. Squeeze out what you need, then tuck the lemon, just as it is, no wrap needed, in the refrigerator's fruit drawer; it will keep for up to a week.

Overripe Strawberries

They may be too squishy to eat out of hand, but past-their-peak strawberries taste great when tossed with honey and slow-roasted until deep red and syrupy, about 1 hour 45 minutes at 300°F. Let cool (syrup will thicken); serve over ice cream, biscuits, or pancakes.

CLASSIC GOOD THING

No-Waste Dressing

Getting that last bit of Dijon mustard out of the jar is a recurring challenge. In April 2006, *Martha Stewart Living* suggested using the jar itself to shake up a tangy vinaigrette. Simply toss in a crushed garlic clove and/or minced shallot along with some chopped fresh herbs—tarragon, for instance. Then pour in balsamic or sherry vinegar, season with coarse salt and freshly ground pepper, screw on the lid, and shake to combine. Add olive oil (four parts oil to one part vinegar); shake again to emulsify. The dressing will keep in the refrigerator for a week; shake before each use.

Crystallized Honey

Crystals indicate quality, not contamination. Dissolve them with gentle heat: Microwave glass jars for 15-second intervals, or warm plastic ones in a pot of water over low heat, shaking often.

**Floral Runner
and Place Cards,**
PAGE 199

5

Entertaining

Pulling off memorable parties takes planning, for sure,
but here's a hint: Some of the most delightful details can also
be the easiest. Turn here for simple ways to add a twist
to cocktails and other beverages; pared-down appetizers made
from just a few companionable ingredients; and desserts
that are both fuss-free and phenomenal (and in some cases, even
portable). Plus, ingenious, budget-friendly ideas for
décor and presentation. Scale up an antipasto platter to
party plank? We're on board.

Host Helpers

CLASSIC GOOD THING

Slipper Basket

Promote a no-shoe policy inside your home by keeping slippers in an attractive basket by the entrance (next to a boot tray, of course, for placing your outdoor footwear). Provide comfortable styles in a variety of sizes for all your guests. Washable ones can be used again and again. This seemingly small step, a *Martha Stewart Living* favorite since February 2002, will do wonders to protect your floors from hard-sole scuffs and also the extra wear and tear that comes when shoes track dirt and grime in from the outside.

Annotated Map

Navigation apps are nice, but highlighting local hot spots on a foldable map is a more personal touch. Use custom "pin" stickers (sold online) or draw symbols on basic dots.

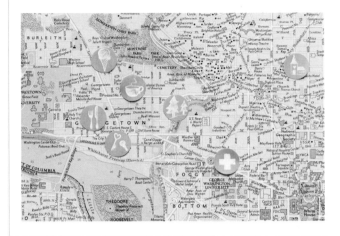

Hospitality Station ❯

Outfit an entryway to make your summer houseguests feel right at home, from the very get-go. This is especially important if you won't be there to greet them when they arrive—or if you've given them the run of the place while on your own getaway. Use the personal touches here as inspiration when laying out your own welcome mat.

1. Hang extra sets of keys so friends can come and go. Retro motel tags are fun and stylish.

2. A framed map of the area is useful and doubles as art. This one is custom calligraphy, available online, but you could design your own (or see above for another idea).

3. Create handy reference binders, putting WiFi passwords and how-to instructions for remotes and the grill into one; slip menus and favorite attractions in another.

Cooking for a Crowd

Platter "Parfait"

Instead of filling a crowd's worth of individual cups, layer fixings—yogurt, seasonal fruit, and a crunchy topping—on a serving dish, family-style. In this tropical twist, fresh pineapple is warmed with brown sugar and oats and sprinkled with toasted hazelnuts and a squeeze of lime. Swap in berries, stone fruits, and apples or pears—cooked or not—and different nuts to suit the season.

Sheet-Pan Pancakes

Make everybody's favorite breakfast without having to do any flipping over a hot stove: Spread your go-to batter—this one has mixed berries folded in—about ¼ inch thick in a rimmed baking sheet that's coated with nonstick cooking spray. Sprinkle with sugar and bake at 450°F until just set, about 10 minutes, then crank up the heat and broil until golden and crunchy on top.

No-Fuss Frittata

Brunch, made easy: Whisk 12 large eggs (to serve 8), fold in fillings, and bake in a buttered 9-by-13-inch dish at 400°F until set, about 18 minutes; lightly brown under the broiler. Serve as a sandwich, slathered with equal parts mayo and Dijon.

Sunday Leftover Lunch

Wow your weekend guests one last time—and send them home with full bellies—by setting out a no-effort afternoon meal. With a little planning ahead, you can build a gorgeous lunch around the remains of other repasts. Just be sure to make more than you need for those, and that all the flavors will ultimately jibe—an easy feat if you follow the "what grows together, goes together" rule. This composed salad, inspired by the classic Niçoise, combines the extra seafood from last night's dinner and hard-cooked eggs with lightly dressed seasonal vegetables.

In-Season Desserts

Rustic galettes are wonderfully simple to assemble and bake, and make an unforgettable impression. Roll out pie dough to an 18-inch round, pile on stone fruit and berries tossed with sugar and lemon juice, and fold pastry over at edges for a casual finish. Chill until firm, then bake at 425°F until crust is golden and juices are bubbling. Cool (about 2 hours) before serving, with sweetened yogurt or crème fraîche.

Better Burgers

Custom-ground meats are surefire grilling game changers. If your mixer doesn't have a grinder attachment, have a butcher do this for you. Then upgrade the condiments—and don't skimp on the bun.

VARIATIONS

1. CLASSIC COMBO: Chuck + Sirloin (equal parts). *Pair with:* cheddar cheese, pickles, ketchup-mayo blend, potato roll

2. STEAKHOUSE SPECIAL: Sirloin + Short Rib (equal parts). *Pair with:* Dijon–grainy mustard mix, blue cheese, grilled onions, lettuce, sesame-seed bun

3. TURKEY CLUB: Turkey Thigh + Bacon (two parts turkey to one part bacon). *Pair with:* lettuce, Swiss cheese, salted tomato, avocado, mayonnaise, English muffin

Grilling Skewers

A grilling basket is not the only way to keep small or unwieldy items from slipping through the grates. Threading multiples of the same food (such as shrimp or cherry tomatoes) on well-soaked skewers keeps them under control, makes turning easier, and allows them to get those telltale grill marks. It also promotes more even cooking. And imagine: You can flip an entire package of franks at once and keep a coil of sausage intact (not so easy to do with tongs alone).

Mix-and-Match Dinner Party

It can be hard to feed a group without leaving anyone out—meatless eaters and those with gluten sensitivities come to mind. You'll also want a flavorful meal that lends itself to advance prep—and, in hot weather, won't heat up the kitchen. This Vietnamese spread ticks all those boxes and scores big on presentation. Set out all the components (research dipping sauce recipes online) and let everyone do their own assembling.

THE MENU

SHRIMP SUMMER ROLLS: Boil 1 pound shrimp; peel and halve lengthwise, and chill. Soak 8 ounces vermicelli in hot water for 30 minutes; drain. Prep shredded Napa cabbage, matchstick carrots, cucumber wedges, dark-green scallion tops (reserve the rest), and Thai basil sprigs. Soften a spring-roll skin in warm water 10 seconds; layer on fillings and roll up like a burrito (see page 149). Repeat to make 20 rolls. Serve with peanut dipping sauce and sambal oelek.

BÁNH MÌ: Grill 1¼ pounds flank steak, then thinly slice against the grain and thread onto 12 to 16 bamboo skewers so guests can grab them. Serve with nuoc cham sauce, toasted baguette (quarter), mint and cilantro sprigs, and extra vegetables from the summer-roll platter.

MANGO SALAD: Toss 2 (underripe) mangoes, peeled and cut into batons, with ½ cup nuoc cham sauce, sliced scallions (from summer rolls), and chopped mint and cilantro. Let stand 30 minutes and up to 2 hours (refrigerated); top with roasted peanuts before serving.

WHAT TO DO IN ADVANCE

- **1 TO 2 WEEKS BEFORE:** Shop for pantry staples and specialty ingredients, such as for the dipping sauces.

- **2 DAYS BEFORE:** Buy produce, beef, and shrimp. Make peanut dipping sauce and refrigerate, covered.

- **1 DAY BEFORE:** Buy baguettes. Boil shrimp. Soak vermicelli. Prep vegetables. Make mango salad and nuoc cham dipping sauce. Refrigerate separately.

- **2 HOURS BEFORE SERVING:** Bring dipping sauces to room temperature. Prepare mango salad. Assemble platters for bánh mì and summer rolls.

- **BEFORE SERVING:** Grill beef and thread on skewers. Toast baguettes. Stir peanuts into mango salad.

Best Practice

ORGANIZED PLATTERS

Eliminate undue stress during the (typically frenzied) lead-up to a big party by plotting out where everything will go ahead of time. Do this the day before or even earlier, in case you find yourself short on serving pieces and need to buy or borrow them in time.

This is especially helpful when hosting a meal buffet-style, where your guests will be invited to help themselves. But even if you'll be doing the dishing out, this planning step can help you avoid any last-minute uncertainty.

Place all the dishes you plan to use on the table, factoring in traffic flow and the order in which the food should be served. Add a sticky note label to each dish and make sure to include utensils.

Tip

To remove all the meat from a lobster tail in one swift motion, insert a fork into the underside and push up. Then chop into bite-size pieces.

Lobster Rolls, Anywhere

Nothing says summer more than the iconic lobster roll, even if you live far from the New England shoreline. Check your local seafood market for live lobsters (and have them do the steaming for you), or order them via one of the many mail-order lobster companies online. Plan on 1 pound of cooked meat (from 5 to 6 pounds of uncooked lobsters) for every six rolls. To assemble, season mayonnaise to taste with fresh lemon juice and coarse salt. Fold in chopped lobster meat. Pile onto toasted buttered split-top rolls—these are as essential as the filling.

REGIONAL SPINS

1. CALIFORNIA: Swap in lime juice for lemon. Fold in chopped cilantro and diced avocado. Serve with lime wedges and more cilantro.

2. CONNECTICUT: Substitute melted butter for mayonnaise and orange juice for lemon. Fold in chopped fresh tarragon; sprinkle more leaves on top.

3. MARYLAND: Stir Old Bay seasoning (and cayenne if extra heat is desired) into mayonnaise mixture. Top roll with melted butter and more Old Bay.

Tip

After extracting meat, place lobster shells and heads in a pot, cover with water, and add aromatics (a quartered onion, celery stalk, and fennel fronds) to make a stock. Simmer until reduced slightly, 2 to 3 hours. Strain; refrigerate up to 3 days or freeze up to 6 months, and use in soups or sauces.

Grilled Cheese Wheel

Here's a crowd-pleasing hors d'oeuvre that you can pull off in no time, especially if you've heated the grill for the main event. You'll want a soft but not runny cheese with a thick rind, such as Camembert or Brie. Brush the rind with olive oil, and grill cheese right on oiled grates over indirect heat until warmed and showing grill marks, about 2 minutes per side (flip with tongs, but don't squeeze!). Serve right away with grilled baguette slices that have also been brushed with oil; these will even keep for up to a day in an airtight container, so you can prep them ahead of time.

Drink Updates

French Press Tea

These svelte appliances are not just for coffee; they also brew multiple cups of tea at once, and with style. Flavor loose-leaf tea with garnishes from your pantry or refrigerator—like cinnamon and fennel seeds with assam (left), and citrus with peppermint (right).

Fast Iced Tea

If you need iced tea on the quick—for unexpected visitors, perhaps, or extra-thirsty party guests—follow this short-steep technique. To make 2½ cups (or four servings), place 3 to 4 tablespoons loose-leaf tea (green is shown here) in the strainer of a ceramic or tempercd-glass teapot. Pour in 2 cups boiling water and let steep 3 minutes, then remove strainer and add 2 cups ice. The cubes will begin to melt—and the tea will reach the ideal strength in a few minutes. Serve in ice-filled glasses.

Fruit Kompot (aka Punch)

If you're looking for a way to give past-its-prime summer fruit new life, try this age-old Eastern European tonic. Mash together 3 pounds of chopped (pitted) stone fruit—peaches, plums, and nectarines work best—with 2 cups mixed fresh berries, ½ cup sugar, and 2 broken cinnamon sticks in a pot; let sit 10 minutes. Add 8 cups water, bring to a boil, and then simmer 10 minutes. Let cool; refrigerate, covered, at least 4 hours and up to overnight. Strain out solids; add fresh lemon juice to taste. Refrigerate kompot in an airtight container up to 1 week. Serve over ice with more fruit. For an extra punch, spike with gin or vodka, or topped off with Champagne.

WAYS TO

MIX IN LEMON FLAVOR

Move over, lemonade—there are zingier ways to perk up cocktails, mocktails, and other refreshers with zesty citrus flavor. Limoncello, lemongrass, lemon sorbet, and preserved lemons? All present and accounted for, along with other up-the-ante ingredients like fresh rosemary and coconut milk.

LIMONCELLO SPARKLER

The lemon-infused Italian cordial—traditionally a *digestivo*—makes a bright, sweet addition to cocktails, including this effervescent concoction: Pour 2 tablespoons limoncello into a chilled coupe. Top with dry prosecco or other sparkling white wine. Serve with a sprig of rosemary.

LEMONGRASS-MINT ICED TEA

A staple of East Asian cooking, lemongrass infuses this tea with a subtle citrusy flavor. For six to eight servings, split 3 lemongrass stalks lengthwise and add to 6 cups water in a pot. Bring to a boil; pour into a large heatproof bowl. Add 6 mint tea bags and ¼ cup honey (or to taste). Let cool completely, then steep in refrigerator overnight. Strain and serve over ice, garnished with a split stalk, if desired.

FROSTY COCONUT LEMONADE

Pink lemonade was the inspiration for this sweet-tart smoothie, which gets a delightfully lush texture from sorbet and frozen fruit (no residual ice shards to contend with). Coconut milk adds flavor and (dairy-free) richness. Purée 1 pint good-quality lemon sorbet with ¾ cup unsweetened coconut milk, ¼ cup water, and ¼ cup frozen raspberries. Divide among four tall glasses and serve.

PRESERVED-LEMON SPRITZER

Most commonly used in North African tagines, preserved lemons are just right for this tangy drink too. (See page 149 or buy a jar at specialty grocers.) Thinly slice 1 quarter of a preserved lemon; muddle in the bottom of a juice glass with 1½ teaspoons superfine sugar until dissolved. Fill glass with ice, then top with seltzer, stir, and serve.

Iced Espresso with Lemon

One more for lemon lovers: This bubbly take on the Italian-American caffè Romano combines the usual espresso shot with lemon soda instead of a simple twist. It's zesty and refreshing—a real eye-opener.

Cold-Brew Coffee

Iced coffee made by quickly cooling a fresh brew can wind up too watery and wan (from all that melting ice). For smoother, more flavorful results, start with a homemade cold-brew concentrate: Stir together 1 pound ground coffee and 8 cups cool water. Cover; let stand at room temperature 24 hours. Strain through a coffee filter or cheesecloth-lined sieve into a jar. Refrigerate, covered, up to a week. See right for serving suggestions.

> ## Coffee Refreshers

1. ICED COFFEE: Dilute 1 part cold brew concentrate with 1 to 2 parts cold water or milk; sweeten as desired (see tip, opposite) and serve over ice. For an extra-cold drink, combine the coffee, milk, and sweetener in a cocktail shaker with ice; shake, and strain into a glass over more ice.

2. ICED CAPPUCCINO: Fill a short glass with ice. Pour in 1 shot cold brew concentrate (or chilled brewed espresso). Sweeten as desired. Top with foamed milk. Dust with ground cinnamon.

3. COFFEE FRAPPÉ: Blend 3 medium scoops vanilla ice cream, 1 cup ice, 1 cup diluted cold-brew concentrate, ½ cup milk, and 2 tablespoons simple syrup in a blender until smooth. Pour into a tall glass. Top with whipped cream, and dust with cocoa powder.

Tip

Simple syrup blends more readily into cold drinks than granulated sugar does. Boil equal parts water and sugar, stirring until sugar has dissolved. Let cool and refrigerate airtight for up to a couple of weeks. Or use sweetened condensed milk, Vietnamese-style.

Flavored Vodkas

Making your own infusions lets you customize your cocktails. Try one of these combos, or experiment with other flavors. Put 1½ cups vodka plus add-ins in an airtight jar and keep in a cool, dark place for a few days, shaking occasionally. Strain before using or storing, up to 1 month at room temperature or 2 months in the freezer.

1. BEET AND HORSERADISH: ½ small beet, sliced + 3 thin slices peeled fresh horseradish

2. CHESTNUT AND DRIED FRUIT: 1 peeled roasted chestnut + ¼ cup mixed dried fruit (raisins, apricots, prunes)

3. STAR ANISE, DRIED CHILE, AND CARDAMOM: 1 star anise + 1 dried chile de árbol + 2 cardamom pods

4. FENNEL AND LEMON: 2 sprigs fennel fronds + 2 thin lemon slices

5. GRAPEFRUIT ZEST AND CORIANDER: 2 strips grapefruit zest + 1 tablespoon coriander seeds, toasted and coarsely ground

6. CELERY AND BAY LEAF: ½ celery stalk + 2 celery leaves + 1 dried bay leaf

7. COFFEE BEAN AND HAZELNUT: 4 coffee beans + 2 tablespoons toasted hazelnuts

Bourbon-Cider Punch

When cidering season kicks in, try this refreshing alternative to the usual warmer—besides being the base ingredient, apple cider is frozen into cubes to chill the drink without watering it down. Combine three parts cider and one part bourbon, add fresh lemon juice and shaved fresh peeled ginger to taste (the spicier the better!) along with thin rounds of a small apple. Stir well and serve over cider ice cubes.

Bloody Marys With a Twist

GARNISH UPGRADES

You can gussy up your go-to Bloody Mary mix with garnishes that double as appetizers—your guests can nibble on the skewers while they sip. Set out rimmed glasses, garnishes, and vodka according to the following suggestions.

1. SHRIMP COCKTAIL: Rim glasses with a lemon wedge and equal parts coarse salt and Old Bay seasoning. Stack skewers with poached shrimp, a lemon wedge, and pitted Castelvetrano (or other) olives. Serve with celery stalks.

2. CAESAR SALAD: Rim glasses with a lemon wedge, flaky sea salt, and grated lemon zest. Stack skewers with chunks of Parmesan, a halved hard-cooked egg, a small anchovy fillet, and a homemade crouton. Serve with romaine leaves.

3. ICEBERG WEDGE: Rim glasses with a lemon wedge and equal parts coarse salt and freshly ground black pepper. Stack skewers with cherry tomatoes, iceberg lettuce, and a firm, creamy blue cheese such as Stilton or Cabrales. Serve with slices of crisp bacon.

SUMMER SPIN

For a warm-weather gathering, lighten things up by replacing the usual Bloody Mary mix with fresh tomatoes, and adding some effervescence. For each serving, pour vodka a third of the way up an ice-filled glass. Squeeze, then drop in, a few cherry tomatoes. Top with seltzer, tuck in some basil sprigs, and add a generous grind of black pepper for a spicy kick.

Tip

Prepare the Bloody Mary mix a day or two before the party to allow the flavors to mingle. Stir it vigorously when ready to serve.

Celery Ice Cubes

Looking for an easy way to shake up your Bloody Mary routine? Freeze tender celery leaves in ice cubes. This is a great way to preserve the flavorful inner leaves after chopping up the stalks for a recipe, and the verdant "rocks" will add a hint of celery flavor to a bunch of other drinks too—think gimlets and tonics. The same idea works with mint, basil, verbena, or edible flowers as well. Freeze the leaves (or petals) in an ice cube tray until solid, then pop the cubes into a resealable plastic bag and use within 6 months.

Melon-Ball Float

Frozen melon balls are a triple whammy, adding bright colors, seasonal flavors, and plenty of chill to party-appropriate (non-dairy) floats. Keep extra orbs in the freezer so you can drop them into pitchers of water, tropical sangria, or your favorite cool cocktail.

1. Use a melon baller to scoop small balls of honeydew and cantaloupe; plan on 4 to 6 balls per serving.

2. Freeze on a parchment-lined baking sheet until firm, at least 4 hours. (You can transfer them to a resealable plastic bag and freeze up to 1 month.)

3. To serve, place several melon balls in a tall glass with 1 or 2 scoops of lemon or coconut sorbet (or one of each).

4. Rub a few mint leaves between your fingers and drop in. Top with seltzer or club soda; serve immediately.

Spiked Watermelon Slushie

In this nod to sgroppino, an icy Venetian cocktail, frozen watermelon flesh stands in for the usual lemon sorbet. Cut 4 pounds peeled seedless watermelon into cubes, and freeze until firm, about 2 hours. Blend until smooth, then add 2 tablespoons vodka and ¼ cup prosecco per 1 cup of slushie.

Ombré Mocktail

Take brunch in a tropical direction with this eye-catching layered (no-tequila) sunrise: Purée a peeled, cored, and chopped pineapple with a pinch of coarse salt. Fill a glass with ice. Pour in ½ cup guava or passion-fruit juice and 1 tablespoon fresh lime juice. Add 2 teaspoons grenadine syrup (don't stir). Gently spoon ½ cup purée on top.

Easy Appetizers

Pâté Update

Proof that the classic spread can be modern, not fusty—and the anchor to a supremely easy and elegant platter. Decant store-bought pâté into a handsome crock, slick with pretty-in-pink raspberry jam, and serve with crostini and a smattering of pickles—select a few from the many small-batch options available (or make your own). It's a salty, sweet, creamy, crunchy crowd-pleaser.

Warmed Olives

Impromptu gatherings, solved: Pick up a variety of olives; a half pound will serve six to eight people (more if the olives are part of a cheese-and-cracker spread). Rinse olives, drain, and place in an oven-proof baking dish. Toss with olive oil and seasonings (as done in this dish, which first appeared in *Martha Stewart Living* in January 2003), such as (from top) hot chile peppers and garlic cloves; bay leaves and fennel seeds; and lemon peel and fresh thyme leaves. Cook 15 to 25 minutes at 350°F, and serve warm.

3-Ingredient Ideas

Base, topping, garnish—these tri-part, no-cook hors d'oeuvres are a cinch to assemble, so you can easily make enough to feed a crowd. Prep the bases in advance: Slice the vegetables and refrigerate, wrapped in damp paper towels inside a resealable bag; toast the crostini and keep in an airtight container at room temperature. Then put them together before your friends arrive.

1. Japanese rice crackers + avocado + salmon roe

2. celery + cream cheese + everything-bagel topping

3. Persian cucumber + Boursin cheese + smoked trout

4. crostini + Major Grey's chutney + serrano ham

WAYS TO
MAKE EASY PAIRINGS

These one-plus appetizers are tastier than the sum of their parts, with additional seasonings unifying the flavors in perfect harmony. With so few ingredients, it's important to buy the best possible quality of each—as in the freshest produce and premium cheese, meat, and toppings.

FENNEL + PARMESAN

Each bite features an unbeatable Italian pairing in a scaled-down (fork-free) package: crunchy, mildly anise-like raw fennel and crumbly, nutty aged Parmigiano-Reggiano. Cut a trimmed fennel bulb into thin wedges, shave cheese over each one, then sprinkle with cracked black pepper and flaky sea salt. Finish with a drizzle of extra-virgin olive oil and snipped fennel fronds.

RHUBARB + BEETS

Meet rhubarb's newest sidekick—beets! Roasting brings out the best qualities of both these vegetables, leaving them tender and not at all bitter. Slice rhubarb on the bias into 2-inch lengths and halve baby beets—these are golden to contrast with the ruby stalks—through their stems. Toss with olive oil; season with salt and pepper. Roast at 375°F until knife-tender. Top with chopped toasted walnuts.

PERSIMMON + BRESAOLA

Do melon and prosciutto one better by cradling Fuyu persimmons in paper-thin slices of bresaola (spiced air-dried beef). The tomato look-alike's honeyed taste plays nicely with the meat's umami, for an unmatched salty-sweet morsel.

DATES + BLUE CHEESE

Stuffed dates have long been part of the appetizer oeuvre. Only here, the usual goat cheese is supplanted by a pungent semi-firm blue such as Gorgonzola Piccante or Spanish Valdeón. Cut a slit into dates—preferably Medjool—and remove any pits; stuff each with a dollop of cheese, then end with a sprinkle of toasted sliced almonds and a drizzle of honey.

Fuss-Free Desserts

Grilled Pound Cake and Peaches

Pound cake and peaches (or other stone fruit) are a favorite summer combo. Do the delightful duo one better by grilling them, for dinner-party status. Brush ½-inch-thick cake slices and halved pitted peaches and plums with melted butter; sprinkle fruit with sugar. Grill, flipping once, until toasted and golden, respectively. Dice the fruit, sprinkle with more sugar along with lime zest and juice, and spoon over cake. Whipped cream is optional though highly recommended.

Chocolate Spoons

These sweet (and stylishly throwback) stirrers elevate after-dinner coffee to dessert course. Just coat the bowl of each spoon with melted bittersweet chocolate, then place them in the refrigerator until you're ready to use them—they'll keep for up to 2 days.

Oven-Baked Churros

Store-bought frozen puff pastry is the shortcut to making Latin American treats that are as crisp and cinnamony sweet as the deep-fried batter originals—and without all the mess. Start by rolling out a package of puff pastry into a rectangle on a floured surface. Brush lightly with a beaten egg. Fold in half and press out air bubbles. Cut crosswise into strips, then twist them into spirals, pressing ends to adhere. Freeze an inch apart on parchment-lined baking sheets to help hold their shape, about 30 minutes and up to a week (covered with plastic wrap). Bake at 425°F until puffed and golden, about 20 minutes. While still hot, toss churros with cinnamon-sugar. Also upgrade standard chocolate sauce (an essential accompaniment) with ancho chile powder and cinnamon to taste.

S'more Variations

When tweaking this campfire favorite, the toasted marshmallow is non-negotiable. Everything else? Up for grabs. Give the following ideas a go, then mix and match to create your own new classics. And of course, keep the original in your rotation too!

1. gingersnaps + lemon curd

2. chocolate wafers + mint-filled chocolate candy (such as Andes)

3. graham crackers + chocolate peanut butter cup

Tip

Put all the fixings on a tray for easy transport, grouping them by category—stack the bases in one section, the melters on another, and the marshmallows in the third. Don't forget the napkins and skewers (or whittled sticks).

Melon-Margarita Pops

No special molds are needed for these handheld treats. Just cut watermelon and cantaloupe into wedges, dip in margarita mix (boozy or not, depending on who's eating), poke with wooden sticks, and freeze until icy. For a pretty presentation, sprinkle the serving dish with peppery (edible) nasturtiums.

Sheet-Pan Ice Cream Sandwiches

The usual method: Baking dozens of cookies, hunting for identical pairs, and forming each sandwich one by one. The new-and-improved way: Bake a cakey cookie dough (it need not be chocolate) in a rimmed baking sheet, layer half with your filling of choice, then cover with remaining cookie half. Freeze until firm, at least a couple of hours and up to a couple of days (covered), then slice into single servings and nestle them in food-safe papers. You can also play around with the fillings, swirling colorful sorbet such as mango and raspberry (shown here) into slightly softened vanilla ice cream.

Tip

For a fun punch, cut top third off a seedless watermelon for the "bowl" and trim bottom so it sits flat. Scoop flesh into a food processor (in batches); puree, then place back into rind and top off with seltzer.

Fools in a Flash

This three-ingredient take on a British fool—a creamy, fruit-compote swirled dessert—is, well, foolishly easy. Instead of making a compote, you simply swap in jam—either a quality store-bought one or a version you've put up yourself. Whisk ½ cup cold heavy cream to soft peaks, fold in 1 cup plain Greek yogurt for a touch of tang, and spoon about a ½ cup of jam evenly on top; gently swirl in, leaving streaks. Divide mixture evenly among four glasses. Refrigerate for at least 1 hour or up to 1 day before serving.

Frozen Terrine

Store-bought shortcut, done right: Line a loaf pan with plastic wrap (leaving overhang for easy unmolding); layer in slightly softened raspberry sorbet, strawberry ice cream, peach frozen yogurt, and melon sorbet (or whatever combination you find appealing), freezing each before adding the next.

Chocolate-Kumquat Bark

Safe to say many folks have never tasted a kumquat, and the citrus's sweet rind and tart flesh definitely have grown-up appeal, so think about introducing it as a cocktail-party confection. The bark is a cinch to make: Spread melted chocolate (dark or semisweet) on parchment, scatter evenly with thinly sliced fruit, and let it harden in the refrigerator. Snap into shards to serve.

Cookie Cups

Serve sorbet or ice cream in cute edible cups that (unlike cones) will catch all drips—and leave you with fewer dishes to clean up. A muffin tin is the trick to getting the cookies to keep their shape. Mix up your favorite roller cookie dough (sugar, gingerbread, or chocolate), then roll out to ¼ inch thick and cut out six 4-inch rounds with a cookie cutter. Mold them around the underside of the tin, alternating cups to keep the cookies apart. Bake according to recipe, and let the cookies cool on the tin. Repeat to make more cups.

Best Practice

CHOCOLATE TIPS & TRICKS

It's one of the most common ingredients and wished-for flavors, so knowing these kitchen-tested pointers will help you prepare chocolate treats like a pro.

1. When baking a chocolate cake, don't flour the pan—dust it with cocoa instead. This way the turned-out layer won't have any white streaks. And when prepping more than one pan, tap the excess cocoa from one into the other.

2. Recipes often call for chocolate to be finely chopped—for example, when it will be melted. With its jagged teeth, a serrated knife will break up the chocolate quickly and easily, without any slippage.

3. For impromptu sweets, consider chocolate cups, which can be filled with peanut butter, as shown, or other fillings (think mousse or fresh berries). Use a small food-safe brush to paint two layers of melted bittersweet chocolate inside small baking liners set in muffin cups. Refrigerate to set, about 10 minutes, before painting on the second layer, and again to finish.

4. Creating your own hot-cocoa blend is easy and lets you avoid unwanted additives: Mix together 2¼ cups confectioners' sugar, 1¼ cups plus 2 tablespoons unsweetened cocoa powder, and ½ teaspoon salt. Store in an airtight jar up to 6 months. To use, stir 1 cup scalded milk into 3 tablespoons cocoa mixture in a mug.

DIY Décor

Herb-Embellished Votives

Grace your table with glass votive holders bedecked with aromatic fresh herbs. Woody herbs are sturdy enough to stand up straight and won't wilt during the party; thyme is shown but rosemary or oregano would also work (as would a combination). Snip the sprigs to match the holder's height, then tie three or four to each one with a piece of twine. When the candles are lit, the herbs will send out wafts of earthy fragrance.

Place Mats for Two

Turn the tables by orienting runners crosswise at each seat rather than down the center. You'll end up with horizontal stripes, and diners will feel connected to their counterparts on the other side. Look for runners in the right dimensions—they shouldn't drop lower than 6 inches on either side (similar to a tablecloth). Or cut and hem a long runner to make two shorter ones.

Color-Coordinated Candles

Go bold with this lively centerpiece, a modern and playful alternative to a blooming display. Purchase brightly hued taper candles—the more, the merrier—and then paint wooden candleholders of varying heights to match. (This is also a good way to unify a mismatched collection.) Stand candlesticks upright on newspaper, outdoors. Spray-paint all around. Let them dry for 10 to 15 minutes. Flip the holders upside down, apply another coat of paint, then let them dry overnight.

Tip

Next time you find yourself with candles that no longer burn, do this: Pop the remaining wax out of its holder, melt it down, and pour it into a smaller votive. Ta-da! You've got a new candle. Follow the steps below for best results. And if combining wax from multiple candles, make sure you use the same type—beeswax, paraffin, or soy.

1. Melt candles in a small pan set over a large pan of simmering water (the melting point of different waxes ranges from 100 to 145 degrees). Remove old wicks with tongs and toss out.

2. Cut a piece of wicking 2 inches taller than votive holder. Knot one end and thread through a wick tab (from a crafts store); tie free end around a wooden skewer. Dip wicking and tab into melted wax to coat. Remove; press tab to bottom of holder. Rest skewer on votive rim.

3. Pour melted wax into votive holder, stopping ½ inch below rim. Let stand until set, 1 hour. To even well at center, pour more wax into center until it's ¼ inch below rim.

Spring Blossoms

Flowering trees in full bloom are a wonder to behold. Alas, their moment in the sun is all too fleeting, so don't just admire them out your window. Bring their beauty indoors, where you—and your guests—can better enjoy it. Large, silky, two-tone magnolia petals are especially striking; trim the branches short so the flowers get as much water as possible. Add an emerging branch that holds a promise of more to come.

Twine Details

This garden go-to is a fitting embellishment for outdoor party accessories. Here are a few ideas.

1. Use twine to tie handwritten labels to pitchers of drinks.

2. Wrap twine around a candlestick or the handles of a serving tray. (Make a few loops, tuck the first end under them; finish wrapping, cut twine, and tuck in end to finish.)

3. Paint names (or write them, with a gel ink pen) on small flat stones, and finish each with a knot of twine, to make placecards.

4. Bundle flatware and napkins together with twine in a casual bow.

Flower Tote

Regular totes just aren't up to the task of cradling fresh bouquets. But with a few basic stitches and supplies, you can turn a plain drawstring bag into a bespoke bloom carrier for the farmers' market—or your own cutting garden. A hole in the bottom allows the stems to peek out; cinch the drawstring to protect delicate petals.

1. Snip bottom seam off bag—this will become the top of the tote. Fold edge in 1½ inches, pin, and iron. To attach strap, pin ends of a 30-inch length of cotton webbing onto opposite sides.

2. Machine-sew a simple straight hem around bag edge. Reinforce strap by sewing a rectangle where webbing and fabric meet.

Arrangement Upgrade

Give a store-bought bouquet of chrysanthemums or other autumn flowers a more lively, spontaneous appeal: Tuck a few foraged specimens—such as the berries and seedheads suggested here—among the blooms. Remove any foliage that will be submerged in water.

1. AMERICAN BITTERSWEET: Bright orange berries

2. CRAB APPLE: Variety of colors (from purple to yellow) and sizes (from pea to clementine)

3. PEEGEE HYDRANGEAS: Mauve-pink cone-shaped flower clusters

4. VIBURNUM BERRIES: Clusters of red or blue berries

5. CLEMATIS SEEDHEADS: Spheres of wispy, hairlike white seeds on stems

1   2   3   4   5

Copper Accents

Conductive copper tape from the hardware store is good for more than electrical jobs. It's also a surprisingly swank (and affordable) way to spruce up glass tumblers, vases, and bottles with graphic patterns. Pick up rolls in different widths to replicate these effects: Repeat the same tape for neat rings, combine different widths, or apply one extra-thick band. First wrap the tape around a vessel to measure and cut it to fit. Then remove the backing and adhere to glass, pressing smoothly as you go. For the bottom bands, tuck the edge of tape underneath.

Café Display

This centerpiece evokes Parisian cafés and their glass-topped tables, under which menus and postcards are often displayed. To create a nature-themed version in your own *maison*, place a sheet of clear polycarbonate (sold at home-supply stores) over a curated selection of prints, fern stems, and feathers or other artifacts. Arrange stones, little pots of moss, and evergreen clippings in jars on top.

Floral Runner and Place Cards

Bring lushness to a spring shower or other special occasion with a peony table display. Unlike taller bouquets, a "runner" of stemmed peonies and galax leaves won't impede the conversation. All you need are floral foam and low dishes, so the flowers appear to float. Matching place cards finish the look.

1. For the runner, cut floral foam to fit a 7-inch-wide shallow dish; add water. Stick leaf stems into foam. Insert two or three peonies on top.

2. For each place-card holder, cut floral foam to fit a 3½-inch-wide shallow dish; follow above directions, except use only one peony. Tuck a handwritten place card inside the flower.

Tip

Peonies are a favorite food of ants. To keep these pests off your table, cut buds before fully open, briefly immerse in warm tap water, and keep stems in water. They'll bloom in a day or two.

Party Plank

An appetizer *abbondanza* like this one is undeniably inviting and artful. But having an all-in-one custom board, cut to the length of your table or sideboard, is also practical, eliminating the need for lots of serving platters and such on the table (and in your sink, post-party).

1. To create the board, have your lumberyard cut a slab to your specifications. Oak, pine, maple, and walnut are all durable options. Then sand it smooth, wipe it clean with tack cloth, and treat it with a food-safe oil, such as mineral oil. Rub it before each use with a wood-treatment cream (also food-safe) to prevent stains.

2. Combine cheeses, charcuterie, fruits, and bread or crackers on the board. Put nuts, olives, and honeycomb in little dishes. Strew the board with herb sprigs and tuck in a few votives.

Hardware Repurposed

Head to your local home-supply store to buy the nuts and bolts of this sparkling and elegant scene. Use a canvas drop cloth for a tablecloth and a long stone tile for a runner. Add metallic hardware—copper couplings for napkin rings, pipe caps and couplings ("with stop") for candleholders, and tube caps for votives. Stay on theme with a copper vase, gold flatware, and copper-colored tapers.

Eco Chic

Going green has never been so colorful, thanks to wooden flatware and bamboo-and-reed plates and bowls (used for the plants)—all of which can be dyed with natural colorings. Dip items in a tub of water tinted with food-safe color or powder dye for up to 30 seconds, then let dry. Double-dip half the plate for an ombré effect. Bonus: The plants double as party favors.

Faux Porcelain

Here's an elegant table display you can whip up on a budget:
Use a couple of cans of spray paint to make a ragtag assortment
of glass bottles and vases look like high-quality porcelain.
Scour your home for jars you can upcycle, use flea-market finds,
and/or buy some mass-market items. Then cover each one with
two or more coats of matte white spray paint, letting them dry
between applications until they are the desired opacity.

Creative Reuse

You don't need a garden's worth of rubber stamps to create these vintage-in-spirit fruit and vegetable motifs. Just repurpose a few corks with different diameters—for example, larger for cherries, oranges, radishes, and peas in their pods, and a smaller one for grapes and blueberries. (Note how the crevices in the cork's surface leave realistic "imperfections" in the produce.) Then draw on the details with fine-tip markers. Besides seasonal party invites and favors, this idea is a great way to personalize stationery and labels for your kitchen creations.

Vellum Revamp

You can make a party's worth of incredibly affordable—and totally portable—decorations with vellum and crafting supplies. Post-bash, fold up the lightweight designs to store.

FOR LANTERN: Cut ten 1-inch-wide strips of vellum, 8 ½ inches long for small lanterns and 11 inches long for large. Stack strips, punch a hole in each end, and secure with mini brads. Fan out to create a 3D shape. Wrap monofilament around one brad; tack to ceiling.

FOR GARLAND: Cut vellum into ¾-by-5-inch strips. Run strips through a sewing machine crosswise, one after the other, until banner reaches desired length. Tack ends to a wall or ceiling.

FOR VOTIVE CENTERPIECE: Cut vellum into rectangles to wrap around votive holders with a 1-inch overlap. Secure ends with double-sided tape; slip sleeves off votives to light candles; replace sleeves.

FOR NAPKIN RINGS: Cut vellum into a ¾-by-5-inch strip. Cut a 1-inch slit lengthwise in one end using a craft knife. Calligraph name on other end. Slip end through slit to make a ring; slide over napkin.

Edged Napkins

With a couple of yards of fabric, spools of contrasting-color thread, and a sewing machine, you can stitch up a stack of elegantly appointed cloth napkins. First, fold each fabric yard into quarters and cut it along creases into four pieces. Then, to mimic a neatly bound, serged hem, set your machine to a zigzag stitch on the smallest possible width. Sew along perimeter, ½ inch from edge, and carefully trim overhang or pull loose threads for a selvage look. Make napkins in multiple patterns and complementary hues, then mix them up for a modern, easygoing setting.

Party & Serving Strategies

Vegetable Bundles

Try this sleeker, single-serve approach to a crudité spread at your next soirée. To make each mini bunch, group thin slices of bell pepper (red, orange, and yellow), carrot, cucumber, red cabbage, pea sprouts, and blanched haricots verts. Tie each cluster with a chive and serve with a tangy dipping sauce (like this bright carrot-ginger number).

Outdoor Drinks Station

Summer entertaining, simplified: Create a streamlined, self-serve refreshment setup that will make your backyard the talk of the town. Take inspiration from this selection: Freshly squeezed lemonade, iced down in a four-gallon stainless-steel dispenser (metal is more insulating than glass), can be enjoyed as is or spiked. Bottles of sparkling water, vodka, and aperitifs (try floral Lillet) are kept on ice for mixing or sipping. An oversize resin Champagne bucket is a step up from a galvanized tin. Glasses are displayed—and easily carried—on a tray (provide an empty tray for used dishes). Garnishes double as décor, with citrus wedges in handsome containers and mint for picking in a tall vessel.

Tip To determine quantities, plan on two drinks per guest for the first hour, then one each per hour after that (one gallon equals 16 eight-ounce drinks).

Sample Starters

Use cute paper condiment cups to dole out sample-size portions of baby Greek salad or a beet-and-radish pairing (toss icicle radishes and sliced roasted beets with olive oil, thyme, and pepper). Add wooden picks (cups and picks sold online).

Citrus Salad

Perk up a winter brunch or holiday open house with this sunny spin on a mixed-fruit salad that features another twist—pomelo, which tastes like grapefruit, only sweeter. Peel, slice into ½-inch-thick rounds, sprinkle with chopped pistachios, and serve with honey and yogurt, for help-yourself drizzling. Ruby grapefruit or Cara Cara oranges would be just as bright and beautiful.

Destination Dogs

Get out of a grilling rut with these guest-worthy franks, which feature regional specialty combinations.

1. BACON-WRAPPED DOG: This griddled wiener is a street-vendor staple in Los Angeles. (The original deep-fried Mexican version is known as a danger dog.) Any sturdy bun will do, so long as it's also grilled; top it with pico de gallo, sliced grilled poblano chile, and cilantro.

2. CHILI DOG: It's the signature beef chili flavored with chocolate and cinnamon that marks the Cincinnati favorite—pile it on thick. Finish with yellow mustard, diced white onion, and lots of finely shredded cheddar on a potato roll.

3. BEER BRAT: Wisconsin (inspired by Germany) is to thank for coming up with the idea of simmering links in beer with sweet onions and caraway seeds before charring on a grill. Serve on a hoagie roll, loaded with sauerkraut and spicy brown mustard, with more beer on the side.

Crudité Cups

Combine produce and dip in individual cups for a portable alternative to a big shared platter—double dipping encouraged! Simply divvy up your dip among small, clear glass cups or (never used) votive candleholders, then fill them with vegetables. Here they're grouped by color, with sliced cucumbers and celery in one cup, carrots and purple endive in another, but you could provide the full spectrum in each serving. Keeping the glasses in an ice-filled tray is both pretty and practical.

Cheesecakes To Go

Carry these adorable desserts to a potluck or group picnic—or send them home with friends after an hours-long gathering. First, divide your cheesecake filling (sans crust) among six 6-ounce flip-top jars, filling each two-thirds full. Place in a deep baking dish; add enough boiling water to reach halfway up sides of jars. Cover dish with foil; cut 6 to 8 slits into top to vent. Bake until set in the center, about 25 minutes. Let cool completely; refrigerate overnight or up to 3 days. Layer with raspberry preserves and graham-cracker crumb "crust" shortly before sealing.

Portable Party

Wicker baskets are fine for a family outing, but if you're aiming for a more elegant picnic or sunset cocktail hour, you'll want something a bit more swanky. Pack up the fixings in shiny tiffin boxes—India's stacking lunch containers—layering crisp vegetables or perishables on top of ice. Improvise on the delicious combos shown here, which include caviar and storebought blini (don't forget the tiny spoon!), crudités and hummus, and steamed shrimp with cocktail sauce and lemon wedges. Skip the plates and tote cocktail napkins and picks in their own tiffin box.

CLASSIC GOOD THING

Quick Chill

Here's a fast and efficient way to cool down wine and spirits from *Martha Stewart Living*'s July/August 2014 issue: Pack a bucket halfway with ice, sprinkle in a handful of coarse salt (it lowers the water temperature), then fill it two-thirds of the way with cold water. Add bottles—they'll be ready to pour in about 10 minutes.

Tip With all due respect to rosé, chilled red wines are also great for summer sipping. Choose fruit-forward, light-bodied varietals that are low in tannins (which make your mouth feel dry and prickly). Think pinot noir, gamay, grenache, and Lambrusco (yes, it's delicious!).

Neater Cheese

Mind your fingers! This simple wrapper makes grate-your-own Parmesan (a must for family-style pasta dinners) a tad more company-friendly. Wrap the larger end of a piece of cheese in parchment, secure it with baker's twine, and rest it and the grater on a plate.

Marzipan-Apricot
Eggs, PAGE 225

6

Celebrating

Making cards and gifts by hand is one of the most
rewarding ways to mark the holidays. Same goes for creating
your own Easter eggs, Halloween costumes, Thanksgiving
place cards, and more. But don't worry about your level of crafting
expertise: The entries here skip complex techniques in favor
of stamps, punches, stencils, and paper folds. And to up the fun,
each one delivers a fresh take on tradition—pom-pom "sparklers"
to wave on July 4th, for example, and champagne cocktails
served with a twist to ring in the New Year.

Valentine's Day

Pom-Pom Valentines

These fluffy cards are as fun to make as they are to share. Use construction paper, scissors, glue, and markers to help kids create simple figures—such as a poodle or pair of cacti—then bring them to life with googly eyes and pom-poms. Extra credit: An alphabet rolling stamp lets kids neatly print a few words at once (with a little spelling help).

Stenciled Treat Bags

Package Valentine trinkets in plain muslin bags, customized with painted hearts or other sweet shapes. For easy stencil-making, use freezer paper: Cut out your own design or use a craft punch, then run an iron over it—the heat will temporarily secure it in place.

TOOLS & MATERIALS

Craft punch or craft knife

Freezer paper

Iron

Muslin bags

Cardboard scrap (cut to fit inside the bag)

Craft paint

Stencil brush

1. Create a stencil by using a craft punch or knife to cut a design into freezer paper.

2. With a dry iron set to medium heat, iron the freezer paper (shiny side down) onto the muslin.

3. Insert cardboard scrap into bag, and then dab craft paint on muslin inside stencil.

4. Carefully peel away freezer paper while paint is still wet (to prevent bleeding).

Heart Animal Cards

Bringing these cute critters to life is child's play—every kid knows how to make a symmetrical heart: Fold construction paper in half, draw half a heart shape aligning with the fold, cut, then unfold. Punch or cut out smaller hearts and other shapes in contrasting paper for fox and panda facial features, then glue in place and draw on any details.

Tip

For a pretty finish, replace the original drawstring with a colorful twine that complements your stencil color.

Punch-and-Link Tags and Toppers

Here's a swell way to add some romance to otherwise plain wrapping: Using a heart-garland craft punch, cut out shapes from colored vellum, then link them together using the tabs and notches. Try alternating colors, layering rows of different shades, or adding a single gold heart to a strand of another color, for a special someone. Wrap the hearts around a package, securing in back with double-sided tape. If desired, write the recipient's name on one of the hearts with a gel pen.

Heartwarming Embellishments

Want to give some cozy winter accessories a personal touch? Not all of us can whip up hand-knitted items with ease, but enhancing a ready-made set is the next best thing: Sew a trio of buttons onto each glove; stitch mini pom-poms along the edge of a scarf; or follow the weave of a knit hat with a contrasting yarn to overstitch a heart or a monogram.

Heart-and-Arrow Pens

Produced assembly-line style, this arsenal of striking pens takes care of gifting for the whole class. Pick up brightly colored gel pens and coordinating papers, gather craft tools and templates (print out ours or sketch your own), and let the kids go to work. Pass out the pens on their own or tucked into matching notebooks with elastic bands.

TOOLS & MATERIALS

Arrow and heart templates (see page 278)

Colored heavyweight paper

Craft scissors

Fringe scissors

Double-sided tape

Capped gel pen

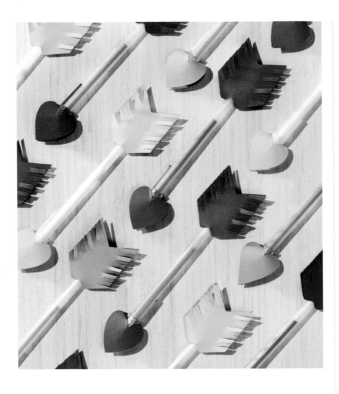

1. Download and print arrow and heart templates (or sketch them freehand). Trace onto paper; cut out with craft scissors.

2. Use fringe scissors to create arrow fletching.

3. Fold each arrow in half, then use tape to attach fletching to end of pen, and heart to pen cap.

Friendship Bracelets

Remember braiding bangles for all your BFFs? With this speedy technique, kids of any age can weave a bunch of bracelets in no time. Knot together six strands each of two colors of embroidery floss at one end; clamp end onto a clipboard. First twist all six strands of each color into one rope, then twist the two colors together and tie the end into a loop for fastening. For gifting: Fold construction-paper hearts as shown to make origami envelopes, sealing with a sticker.

Potted Plants

Succulents (or other small houseplants) make long-lasting gifts for co-workers, teachers, or other deserving folks. What makes these specimens extra special are their pretty "pots"—made in multiples from inexpensive wooden cups (sold online). First, cut or punch a heart shape out of stencil film, then stick the film onto a cup. Dab craft paint on stencil with a small paint brush; peel off while paint is wet. Let dry, then slip in a plant—and care instructions.

Candy Tins

These designs have modern style, but they're made with a blast from the past—an inexpensive toy called a Spirograph. It works by spinning a gearlike wheel inside a plastic ring using the tip of a pen to create intricate patterns, like the ones made on these candy-filled window tins. Remove clear plastic insert from lid; trace it onto colored paper. Use a white gel pen to create a Spirograph design, leaving room for a message or hand-drawn heart. Replace insert and place paper against it.

Marshmallow Hearts

Hot chocolate is always appreciated, but here's how to really bring the love: Use a sharp knife to cut a marshmallow (any size works, including minis) in half crosswise, to make two circles. Snip one side in the middle with kitchen shears, then pinch the opposite side for the point. Float hearts atop steaming cocoa.

Cookie Envelopes

With its freezer-paper lining, each one of these pretty hand-folded parcels can hold an oversize (3-inch) treat—no grease or smudges.

1. Cut a 7-by-7-inch square of freezer paper, and another of patterned medium-weight paper, such as origami paper.

2. Place patterned paper square on work surface, pattern-side-down; top with freezer paper. Fold each corner of combined square in, so all four points meet in center.

3. Tape along two bottom seams; insert cookie.

4. Tape down top flap and attach a label and/or twine ribbon, if desired.

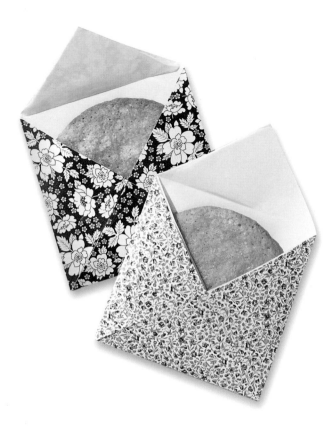

Tempering Chocolate

If you're making truffles for Valentine's Day, tempering the chocolate they'll be dipped in is the only way to get that glossy sheen to last. Precision is key—employ a candy thermometer to gauge the temperature. Chop chocolate with a serrated knife. Reserve one-fifth; place the rest in a heatproof bowl. Bring an inch of water to a simmer in a saucepan (large enough to rest the bowl on top, without the bottom of the bowl touching the water); turn off heat. Rest bowl on pan, stirring gently with a heatproof silicone spatula as chocolate melts. Check temperature frequently; when it reaches 118°F, remove bowl from heat. Add reserved chocolate and stir until mixture cools to 84°F. Place bowl back over simmering water; stir until it reaches 88°F to 90°F. Use immediately.

Edible Valentines

Heart-shaped cutters are not just for cookies. Here are some other ideas:

1. Sauté firm polenta hearts until golden.

2. Cut bread into hearts for French toast.

3. Add thin, roasted-beet hearts to a salad.

4. Cut baked brownies, wiping cutter and coating with nonstick spray as needed.

5. For easy ravioli, fill wonton wrappers as desired, then seal and cut before boiling.

6. Slice raw carrots into ¼-inch rounds, then cut out hearts and simmer in soup.

7. Bake heart-shaped chocolate cookies for strawberry ice-cream sandwiches.

8. Punch out cherry (or raspberry) scones into hearts before baking.

9. Tint gelatin with pomegranate juice or pink lemonade; let set, then cut.

Easter

Easter Daffodils

A symbol of rebirth, these spring blooms are definitely holiday-worthy, especially when arranged in a modern display like below (*Martha Stewart Living*, April 2009). Tie pieces of raffia (dyed yellow for added cheer) around the stems, near the top, to keep them upright and the blooms in a neat ball (cut stems so ends are even). Stand in a clear vase.

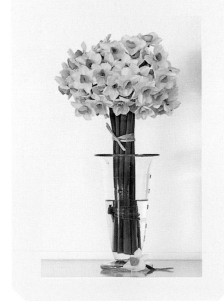

Greener Grass

Wheatgrass makes a real-life, eco-friendly alternative to faux nesting material for an Easter basket. You can buy a flat from a nursery and cut it to fit your container, but it sprouts up so fast—full and lush in a couple of weeks—why not just grow it yourself?

1. Buy seeds at a natural-food or garden store. Soak for 6 to 12 hours.

2. Set the seeds atop ½ to 1 inch of moist soil in a plastic tray; set it inside your basket. Cover and keep out of the light. Spray daily with water. The seeds should germinate in about 2 days.

3. When grass is 1 to 2 inches tall, uncover and move to indirect sunlight. Continue spraying daily. It should take about 12 days total to grow to 6 inches.

Stamped Eggs

Kids will adore "stamping" natural or dyed eggs with everyday materials: bubble wrap for dots, corrugated cardboard for stripes. (And you'll love upcycling these packaging items rather than tossing them.) Just brush matte acrylic paint in a smooth coat across a sheet of either material, then slowly roll egg across it.

Marbleized Eggs

These eggs only look extravagant. The two-step, no-mess technique is sure to become a favorite, because it's easy, and every egg looks different from the last. First, dye eggs solid colors; let dry, 15 minutes. Prep other dyes in darker or different shades; add one tablespoon olive oil to each. Stir with a fork to create swirls of oil, add a dyed egg, and roll it around to pick up streaks. Remove, blot with a paper towel, and let dry.

Neon Eggs Two Ways

Fluorescent eggs will be easier to hunt down—and garner more raves—than their pastel counterparts. Start by dyeing your eggs in bolder-is-better colors. Then give them sparkles or stripes (or both). For sparkles: Brush half an egg with craft glue, and sprinkle with glitter in same shade. Place egg glitter-side-up to dry. Repeat on other side. For stripes: Hold the loose end of a spool of thread in a contrasting neon shade against egg with your finger. Wrap thread around egg, securing loose end with loops as you work; tack periodically with Mod Podge. Snip thread from spool, then tuck the end under and glue in place.

Bunny Place Settings

What came first, the Easter bunny or the egg? Both are front and center in these super-cute place settings, which kids can help make. For each setting, you'll need a starched and ironed square linen napkin—this one is 20-by-20 inches but a smaller one works too—along with a ribbon, black paint marker, and hard-cooked egg, dyed or left natural.

1. Fold the napkin into thirds.

2. Grasp lower corners on long side of folded rectangle, and fold them up to meet in center, creating a paper-airplane shape.

3. Flip over napkin so seam faces table. Fold in outer edges to meet in center.

4. Place egg on pointed napkin tip, tie "ears" above it with ribbon, and nestle egg into place. Draw on eyes, nose, and whiskers with marker.

WEEKEND PROJECT

No-Waste Nests

A nest that would fit in the palm of your hand, crafted from shredded paper—recycle packing material or shred your own—is just right for doling out jelly beans and candy eggs.

TOOLS & MATERIALS

Small balloons

Small jars

Découpage finish

Small paintbrush

Shredded paper

1. For each nest, blow up balloon to desired nest size (these are 3 to 5 inches across). Rest balloon on jar, knotted-end down.

2. In a small dish, mix equal parts découpage finish and water to make a glue. Brush mixture onto top half of balloon to create a guide for nest.

3. Lay strips of shredded paper onto glue-covered area, covering it as much as possible.

4. Dip small handfuls of crumpled shredded paper in glue mixture, and continue adding to create a full nest. Let dry overnight.

5. Pop balloon. Top off inside of nest with more shredded paper; fill with treats.

Origami Egg Holders

With some basic folds, you can create paper egg cups for your holiday table. Get the kids in on the action, or make one for each person to use when egg decorating; or write names on dyed shells and let the holders double as place cards. Choose paper with a different color or pattern on each side. Start by folding the square in half, then follow the steps as shown.

1

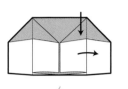

2

3

4

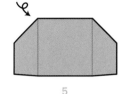

5

6

7

8

9

Marzipan-Apricot Eggs

Prepare to delight the grown-ups at your holiday table: Each sparkly pastel shell holds a dark chocolate–stuffed dried Turkish apricot in its center. Set a few at each place setting, or package as parting gifts. With a paring knife, make a ½-inch-wide pocket on side of each dried apricot. Stuff with a ¼-by-½-inch piece of dark chocolate. Pinch off a teaspoon of marzipan; flatten with your fingers to ⅛ inch thick. Wrap around apricot, molding to adhere and forming an egg shape. With a small brush, coat eggs with beaten egg white; roll in colored sanding sugar. Let set 30 minutes. Store airtight up to 2 weeks. Note: Raw eggs should not be consumed by pregnant women, young children, the elderly, or anyone with compromised health.

Passover

Matzo Pie Crust

For a seder-friendly swap, use matzo in place of graham-cracker crumbs to make a press-in-the-pan pie crust. Pulse four to six sheets matzo in a food processor until finely ground (you should have about 1½ cups). Add ¼ teaspoon kosher salt, ⅓ cup melted coconut oil, ¼ cup sugar, and 3 tablespoons tap water. Pulse to combine, then press into the bottom and up the sides of a 9-inch pie plate. Bake at 350°F until light golden, 16 to 18 minutes. Let cool completely before filling.

Zesty Matzo Snack

Make plain matzo into a snappy pre-dinner nibble—or turn a leftover supply into tasty snacks once the holiday is over. Brush each matzo cracker with a beaten egg white, then sprinkle with a heaping teaspoon (or to taste) of your favorite seasoning, such as za'atar, harissa spice, sesame seeds, or a mix of dried dill and celery seeds. Season with flaky sea salt and bake in a 350°F oven until fragrant and dry, about 10 minutes. Let cool slightly, then break into bite-size pieces to serve.

Seder Plate Settings

For a modern spin on the Passover plate, incorporate new ingredients that symbolize liberation today. An orange, for example, represents solidarity with all marginalized people. Other ideas: olives for peace, fair-trade coffee or chocolate for workers' rights.

Mother's Day

Paper Tulips

Reminiscent of the real beauties and sure to last and last. Plus, these folded-paper incarnations double as greeting cards when you write a message for Mom on the leaves. Make a single stem or a bountiful bouquet—in one color or a whole peppy rainbow.

TOOLS & MATERIALS

Medium-weight colored papers

Double-sided tape

Scissors

Cloth-covered floral wire

Craft glue

Tip

This idea works for other occasions too—think Valentine's Day (say, for teachers) or as a get-well-soon sentiment.

1. Cut out a square piece of paper 5 inches or larger. Fold in half, open, then fold in half the other way; unfold.

2. Apply an inch-long strip of double-sided tape alongside each of the four creases; pinch so each piece of tape adheres and paper pops up into a cupped shape.

3. With scissors, cut edges into a petal shape. Poke a small hole in bottom of folded flower.

4. Fold over tip of wire, insert into bottom of flower, and glue to secure.

5. With scissors, cut out paper leaves; write messages on them. Glue leaves onto wire.

Balloon Bouquet

Surprise Mom this year with a bunch of helium-filled balloons in pretty colors—then personalize the bundle with her "name" spelled out below. Trace letter stencils (or draw your own designs) onto card stock, cut them out, and punch a hole in the top of each. String the letters from three balloons with baker's twine. Fasten the bouquet to a favorite chair or another special spot.

Heart Photo

Even if your generation only acknowledges digital, a framed, printed photo is still en vogue for Mom—especially when you add a cross-stitched heart "emoji." Print out a picture she will love in matte black-and-white (so the red heart shows). Place the heart template (see page 278) on the picture, poke holes through the grid with a thick straight pin, and use red embroidery floss and cross-stitches to connect the dots. Frame to finish.

Care Package

Kids aren't the only ones who can shower Mom with appreciation on her special day. For a grown-up gift box from her plus-one, snag a collapsible cardboard carrier, available online or at crafts stores. Fill it with a vase of fresh flowers—peonies, roses, and sandersonia are shown here—and a bottle of (pink!) Champagne. Tuck in chocolates or bath salts and a handwritten note, and wrap the whole thing in an ombré ribbon (she'll really appreciate this little detail).

Tip

When piercing the grid holes, tuck a piece of cork or cardboard underneath the photo to protect your work surface. You can find inexpensive cork rounds at crafts stores—they double as trivets.

Father's Day

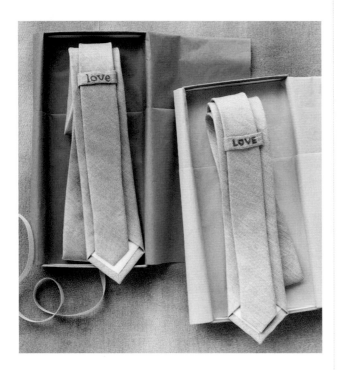

Embroidered Tie

Ties are old hat as gifts for dear old Dad, but not when hand-stitched with a heartfelt sentiment for only him to see—like love or XOXO. Hint: It will be all the more meaningful if kids do the stitching themselves.

TOOLS & MATERIALS

Disappearing-ink fabric marker

Linen or cotton necktie

Embroidery floss

Needle

Fabric scissors

1. Write message on the fabric loop on back side of tie with fabric marker.

2. Separate two or three strands of embroidery floss; thread needle. Go over letters with small chain or stem stitches.

Book Boxes

Appeal to a literary dad's sense of order by giving him organizers disguised as artful books. Make a few—say, one from each kid—for holding different items. Stain the surface of a wooden book box (sold online) with diluted multi-surface craft paint; let dry. Add designs like diamonds and stripes with undiluted paint, using stencils or painters' tape to ensure straight lines. Line the inside compartment with decorative paper—or velvet for cushioning cuff links and watches. Tuck in a few shared mementos to start his collection.

Key Fobs

Dad will never misplace his keys again after he receives one of these stylish gizmos, made from sturdy hooks and carabiners from a hardware store (or even scavenged from his own toolbox). You'll also need colorful leather cord or washi tape, superglue, and scissors. Begin by snipping a double length of cord. Glue loose ends side by side to hook; flip hook over and begin pulling cord through to create a series of knots for a braided look (below left). Or simply wrap a single length of cord or washi tape around hook for a smoother effect. Snip other end; glue to secure.

Custom Cookies

For a sweet surprise, bake his favorite cut-out cookies (these are lemon poppy seed) to spell D-A-D. Using letter cookie cutters (or your own templates), cut letters from rolled-out dough with a paring knife, making twice as many Ds as As. Stack in a bakery-tissue-lined box; tie with twine.

Personalized Coasters

Cork coasters come in inexpensive packs, so you can embellish a whole set (without sweating any mistakes). Create stripes with masking tape and initials with vinyl letters. With a stencil brush, apply craft paint; let dry. Peel off guides.

Fourth of July

Batik-Inspired Table Linens

For stylish, summery linens on a budget, try ice-dyeing—this foolproof technique gives a solid tablecloth or set of napkins a subtle watercolor-like wash that's right at home at a backyard bash. Place a wire rack over a plastic bin (or in a sink). Soak fabric in water, then twist and bend it into a snake shape to fit on rack; this will create a wave pattern. Gather fabric into center of rack; cover with ice cubes. Sprinkle blue powder dye evenly on top; let ice melt. To set the color, wash and tumble-dry the linens (separate from other laundry).

No-Sew Stripes

It takes only a few minutes to fashion stitch-free table décor (from *Martha Stewart Living*, July/August 2019) using grosgrain ribbons, heat-bond adhesive, and an iron. For a runner, embellish a length of linen in a complementary shade: Cut ribbon and a strip of adhesive to required length, put adhesive under ribbon at edge of fabric, and press with a hot iron to attach it. Then add a couple of bands to napkins following the same process. For even more patriotic panache, tie up bundles of flatware for each place setting using the same or another ribbon with coordinating stripes.

Spirited Sprays

For an Independence Day arrangement, gather red, white, and blue blooms, such as red and blue anemones, true-blue alliums, blue larkspur, and white phlox in an outdoor-friendly vessel, such as this enamelware cup. Add extra blooms in other shades of the same colors to build depth. Keep the water cool (replenish as needed) to make it last.

Easy Glassware Upgrades

Here's a neat trick for making plain glass tumblers and pitchers more guest-worthy for a summer shindig: Slip on red and/or blue rubber bands in a variety of widths. Besides adding festive flair, the bands provide a slip-proof grip.

Pom-Poms

These festive "sparklers" let all ages get in on the fun. For each, fold a sheet of tissue paper into thirds vertically. Cut one edge so you have 3 stacked strips, then fringe them using a fringe cutter, along one long side. Repeat with 2 more sheets of tissue. Cut a strip of silvery Mylar paper to match tissue. Layer segments; starting at one short end, roll stacked paper, below fringe, onto end of a wooden dowel, securing with double-sided tape as you go. Cut a cone of card stock. Wrap around base of pom-pom; tape to secure.

Red and White Ices

This refreshing salute to Old Glory is all about the assembly. Put lemon and raspberry ices in single-serve food-service cups (look for compostable ones online). Arrange in alternating rows on a parchment-lined baking sheet. Freeze the sheet until ready to serve. Stack blue cocktail napkins for the "stars."

Tip Use one of the cups to hold spoons— these eco-friendly wooden ones have classic ice-cream-parlor appeal.

Pull-Apart Sliders

Individual sliders are fine, but these melty self-serve ones are much more fun for a crowd. Broil (or grill) 12 mini patties. Slice a 12-pack of Hawaiian sweet rolls in half horizontally. Tuck broiled patties inside, between layers of cheese; brush buns with melted butter, sprinkle on sesame seeds, and bake at 350°F for about 10 minutes. Spear each slider with an LTC (lettuce, tomato, cornichon) skewer.

Bespoke Bike

For a bright, festive (and night-safe) alternative to the usual streamers and pinwheels, wrap a strand of LED lights around your bike's frame. Then take it out for a spin!

Flag Toppers

Want to make any cake (or cupcake, or cocktail) Fourth of July–ready in a snap? Plant a flag in it. Pick one grosgrain ribbon design or use a medley of sizes and prints, as below. For each topper: Brush 3-to-5-inch pieces of ribbon with fabric stiffener (like Aleene's); lay them over pencils to form the ripples, or markers for bigger waves. (Prevent sticking by laying plastic wrap between ribbon and tools.) Let set overnight; hot-glue them to wooden skewers in varying heights.

Red, White, and Blue Layer Cake

A cake that stands tall (see right) commands center stage. But this one also comes with a spirited "reveal" in every slice, thanks to colorful fruit fillings. Trim and halve two 8-inch round cakes horizontally. Fill a pastry bag with ½ cup white buttercream. Pipe frosting around perimeter of one layer. Combine 1 cup small blueberries and 6 tablespoons blueberry jam; spread inside border. Place another layer on top; spread with 1 cup buttercream. Add third layer; pipe a frosting border. Combine 1 cup finely sliced strawberries and ¼ cup strawberry jam; spread inside border. Top with last layer. Spread a thin coat of frosting over top and sides. Chill 30 minutes. Frost with final coat; serve.

Instant Whipped Cream

Try this neat trick at a picnic, or anywhere an electric mixer is not an option: Fill a jar a quarter of the way with cold heavy cream. Firmly screw on the lid, then shake vigorously (as you would a cocktail) until thick and silken, 2 to 3 minutes. Serve with fresh berries.

Halloween

Eerie House Numbers

The devil is in the details, and even tiny touches can have a terrifying effect. Take this gruesome trick: What appears to be blood oozing from your abode is actually tinted hot glue. Squirt the red glue directly onto the edges of your house numbers (or mailbox, or letter slot), blowing on it to speed up cooling and help control the drops. Come November 1, simply peel off the glue, leaving behind no evidence.

Anatomical Arrangement

It's always good to have an extra pair of hands when assembling your Halloween décor. These bony appendages (actually, articulated model hands that can be found online) are just the thing to hold your taper candles: Hot-glue clear candlesticks or bud vases in their grasp, or just prop the skeletal extremities in place. For the real showstopper, replicate this blood-red, exploding-brain bouquet with smoke bush, Black Beauty roses, alliums, and cobra lilies in a glass vessel, then set it inside a model skull with a detachable top and spacious cranial cavity.

No-Carve Pumpkins

Good ol' jack-o'-lanterns have their place in the Halloween canon, but there are other ways than carving pumpkins to create a dramatic, diabolical display. (And because there are no sharp tools, even little kids can get in on the action.) Visit a local pumpkin patch to find an eerie assortment of gourds, like the ghostly white and blue specimens shown here (which include gnarly Hubbards). Pile them on and around a bench in your foyer or a front porch to accommodate your design. Then draw the outline of a stark tree over several of them with a grease pencil; fill in the shape using a brush and matte black craft paint. Paint a real branch (look for a scraggly one) and mount it above—and finish with a faux crow perched among the phantom limbs.

House-Number Gourd

These front-porch greeters, which first appeared in *Martha Stewart Living* in October 2007, offer form and function over frights, and let guests know they've arrived. Print your address digits in desired font and size. Cut out, and tape to a large dried gourd (available from florists or online; this one is a "jumbo soccer ball" variety).

Fit a wood-burning tool (an inexpensive crafter's tool sold online) with a needle tip; pierce evenly spaced holes into gourd's skin, outlining numbers. Add flourishes with a pencil; pierce their outlines. Arrange with pear gourds, as here.

Faux Front Door

This petrifying paw looks like an innocent prop. But once trick-or-treaters approach, watch out! The hand (e.g., you) will playfully grab at anyone who dares reach for an extra piece. Chalk the details of a door on black kraft paper and tape it to your real door's interior frame. Cut a hole in the middle that's just big enough to fit your arm (covered in mummy tape or a werewolf costume), and place candy below.

Lurid Lab

This creepy collection could only belong to a mad scientist-slash-party host. Your guests would have to get frightfully close to discover that the phosphorescent specimens are actually biology-class anatomy cards: Slip animal and insect X-rays (found online) into glass containers, then drop in a flameless candle to illuminate each one.

Ghoulish Grub

Treat your guests to a macabre feast inspired by the underworld and presented on ominous black dishware.

1. GARDEN-OF-EVIL PUNCH: Freeze deeply colored fruits—kumquats, husk cherries, red grapes, and pomegranate seeds—in an 8-inch cake pan, filled halfway with water until solid. Unmold and float atop your favorite (spiked!) pomegranate punch. Add edible hibiscus and begonia leaves if desired. Ladle into glasses; top with seltzer.

2. GRISSINI SNAKES + DARK-NIGHT DIP: Use black tahini, such as Kevala Organic, instead of regular to make a dark spin on baba ghanoush. For the grissini: Divide a batch of pizza dough in two; tint half with squid ink (or black gel-paste food coloring). Roll pieces into squiggly ropes; bake at 400°F until crisp.

3. TELLTALE HEARTS: Trim dried figs into heart shapes by cutting a notch in the rounded end of each, then stuff with goat cheese, wrap in prosciutto, skewer with picks, and drizzle with balsamic vinegar.

WAYS TO
MAKE COSTUMES

A few simple techniques and a black base layer let you skip the pop-up Halloween store (and its cookie-cutter offerings) and create one-of-a-kind costumes for the whole clan. Just grab some fun materials—feather trim! false eyelashes!—and whip up these DIY disguises.

BAT BOY

Transform an inexpensive ski hood and arm warmers with cut-to-fit ears and wings so your nocturnal crusader can take flight. Cut triangle ears out of stiffened black felt, and wings out of regular black felt. Curve the triangles, then attach to the hood by hand with a running stitch. Attach felt wings to arm warmers by hand with a running stitch.

LADYBUG

Good luck will be on your side when you whip up this cute getup. Glue extra-large faux eyelashes onto big black sunglasses. For each feeler, twist pairs of black pipe cleaners together; stick their wires into a black pom-pom. Wrap opposite ends of feelers around headband; twist to secure. Peel backing off black felt adhesive circles and stick on a red dress. Finish the look with black top, tights, and ballet slippers.

BLACKBIRD

This shimmering cape is something to crow about. To gauge cape length, measure from base of wearer's neck to intended hem—this chic wrap hits above the elbow. Purchase felt yardage in twice cape's length. Cut a semicircle of black felt; notch center of straight side (for neck). Hot-glue on overlapping rows of feathered trim, from bottom up. Hot-glue velvet ribbon around neck. Don feather false eyelashes.

GLITZY GUPPY

Grab your hot-glue gun to turn a dancer into a goldfish. Cut off top 6 inches of a tutu; cut this in half. Glue pieces to leotard arms. Glue remaining tutu to bottom of leotard, from inner part of one leg opening to the other. Glue overlapping rows of sequins onto leotard and shoes. For headband: Glue white pom-poms to orange pom-poms; glue a black sequin pupil to each. Glue small tutu pieces around orange pom-poms.

Bountiful Buffet

Rather than trying to make room for the turkey and all the fixings on the dining table (always a feat), set a scene of abundance by putting everything on a buffet. This way you can invite family and friends to partake as they please—no interrupting the conversation to pass the gravy. Present the various offerings in dishes of varying heights and textures. Include a few embellishments, such as a brass candleholder and a towering, wilt-proof arrangement of foraged grasses and seed heads in a burnished pitcher.

Thanksgiving

Notes of Gratitude

Here's a fun—and interactive—way to remind everyone what the holiday is all about: Write out "I'm thankful for..." on colored cards with a white or metallic gel pen—or have the kids do it. Put a card on each place setting, along with more pens so guests can jot down their answers. Once cards are complete—and collected on a dedicated platter—have each person pick a card to read out loud. Everyone else can try to guess who wrote the message, or just let the sentiment spark a new conversation.

Corn Husk Wreath

Craft this rustic nod to the harvest season—and the sun—from humble, grocery-store tamale wrappers.

TOOLS & MATERIALS

Corn husks

Bowl of water and paper towels

Straw wreath

T pins

Glue gun

Scissors

1. For a base layer, dunk corn husks in water, blot slightly on paper towels, and wrap snugly around wreath, overlapping edges to cover straw entirely. Secure undersides of husks with T pins.

2. To shape radiating husks: Dunk husks in water, blot slightly, and temporarily pin to wreath so they dry naturally in curled or undulating shapes. Go around the wreath, creating several layers. Let dry.

3. Permanently attach radiating husks a few at a time, positioning them as you like and using glue gun to secure. Attach in layers, tucking additional husks behind until you reach desired fullness. As you go, use scissors to trim husk lengths and widths.

Simplest Centerpieces

Grasses like bunny tail (far left) and timothy (far right) are tall, thin, and airy enough for conversation to flow through. Keep the scene modern by sticking to one monochromatic variety per vase and arrange each in a loose lineup. The spare aesthetic will last all winter long. Just change the containers for an instant refresh.

Wreath of Grain

Ombré goes au naturel with dried botanicals. Wire single-shade bundles onto a metal form, from bottom to top—and light to dark. Tuck in longer grasses and fronds for added lushness; finish with a coordinating ribbon.

Candle Hurricanes

Wrap glass vessels with a variety of dried ferns and other foliage to provide flickering light by night and farmhouse-chic décor by day. Dot hot glue along a leaf's spine, then gently press it around the exterior of a hurricane. Enhance the display with other botanicals, like the spray of frosted explosion grass in the background.

The Kids' Table

If your holiday guest list includes a gaggle of kids, ward off the inevitable questions ("Is it ready yet?") and complaints ("I'm bored!") by setting out a selection of activities that doubles as table décor. You can start with the following four ideas, then let them inspire your own delaying distractions.

1. GAMES: Turn a runner into a gaming station (with tic-tac-toe and checkers) with fabric paint and stencils. Paint or stamp wooden rounds for the pieces.

2. DRAW-ON DOLLS: Place an old-school wooden figurine (complete with acorn cap and scarf) at each setting; provide markers so kids can fill in the features.

3. LETTERS: Use alphabet tiles for "place cards." Encourage kids to swap them, spell out (or make up) new words, and take them home as mementos.

4. DIY JEWELRY: Set out dishes with necklace- or bracelet-making supplies, such as cords and beads. Kids can keep or share their creations.

Trivia Quiz Booklet

Celebrate family and friends with a game that sparks conversations about everyone's past and present. Follow the template instructions on page 278 to make booklets with the desired number of questions. Have people fill them out before the meal, then go through the answers as a group. To keep the tradition fresh, change the focus from year to year. For example, you could match up family members with their claims to fame, or dig up old photos to accompany the questions. The best part? The booklets double as keepsakes.

Makeshift Menu

Whet your guests' appetites by writing out the holiday menu, café-style, on a roll of brown kraft paper (a rustic spin on the typical chalkboard). Jot the name of each dish with a marker, then thread a length of sturdy twine through the paper's tube. Suspend from a small nail or picture hook (or removable adhesive hanger) over a buffet table or wherever your guests will be gathering.

Tip If you're short on time, buy small blank notebooks and write the questions—no printing needed.

4

WAYS TO

MAKE
PLACE CARDS

With so much attention being paid to the meal, it's easy for hosts to overlook the other niceties of entertaining, such as place cards. Fortunately, these are simple and can help create a more welcoming scene. A couple will even keep little hands busy until the feast is served.

EMBROIDERED LEAVES

Stitch your guests' names onto sturdy leaves, such as these sizable magnolia specimens. They'll need to dry for a few days after embroidering (to hold their shape), so plan ahead. Set leaves upside down on a work surface, veins facing up. Write a name on each leaf using a metallic marker. With a plastic needle and thick thread, go over the letters in a basic backstitch; overlap the stitches slightly for a rustic look.

TAMALE WRAPS

These "place cards" double as favors: They look like savory tamales but in fact hold a sweet surprise of chocolate-covered espresso beans (or jelly beans, for kids). Fill each corn husk with treats, twist it closed, and secure it with double-sided tape at one end and a thin strip of husk at the other. Tie paper slips at the tops, inscribed with guests' names. If you like, add a message of gratitude as well.

PRESSED-LEAF ANIMALS

Autumn leaves (you can purchase pressed ones, or gather some from the backyard) are the basis of this kid-friendly craft. Place an animal template (see page 280) on each leaf, secure it with double-sided tape, and use detail scissors to cut out the shape. Reinforce brittle leaves with layers of tape on the backs before cutting them. Write names on the place cards with a silver paint pen.

GOBBLER POP-UPS

Here's another fun idea for your young guests: Make pop-up turkeys. Set out crafts-store supplies and demonstrate the first one. Start by cutting out heavyweight paper into squares. Stick a honeycomb ball onto each one. Draw on turkey feathers and a face with colored pencils and crayons and finish by writing the person's name in a corner. Set the card on a square napkin for a geometric backdrop.

Dessert Table Décor

If you've delegated the pies, your dessert table might be a bit of a hodgepodge of pans. Unify them by encircling each one with a ring of greenery. Gather pretty foliage (such as the eucalyptus, bay, and olive leaves shown here), twist them into wreaths—each just wider than the pan it will frame—and put in position.

Mini Pie Parcels

Some guests are known for filling up on the turkey and sides, leaving no room for dessert. Plan ahead so you can send them on their way with individual pies baked in 5-inch aluminum tins.

1. Prep fabric for wrapping ahead of time: Cut 17½-inch squares. Press edges under ¼ inch, then another ¼ inch. Hem all the way around. (Or use store-bought napkins.)

2. Wrap each pie in waxed paper or parchment, secure with twine, then center atop a fabric square. Drape opposite corners over pie, then tie remaining corners in a square knot.

Pie Dough

One of the trickiest parts of working with rolled-out pie dough is getting it from the work surface to the pie plate. But even novices can manage this task by using this pro tip from the November 2012 issue of *Martha Stewart Living*: Roll the dough around the pin, from one side to the other, then gently lift and unroll it over the dish. (If the dough is too soft, chill it for 15 minutes so it won't stick.) Gently pat dough into place and trim excess with kitchen shears, leaving a 1-inch overhang; fold dough under to reinforce edge.

Leaf Trivets

Protect your dining table and add a little seasonal panache in the process, with these fetching trivets. Trace a leaf template (see page 281) onto a corkboard tile (from an office-supply store) with a marker. With corkboard on a cutting mat, cut along outline with a craft knife. Turn over to display. Bring an extra one for your hostess, under your Thanksgiving dish.

Foolproof Presentation

For a platter that's equal parts pretty and practical, skip bringing the whole turkey to the table, opting instead to do the carving (and curating) in the kitchen. After all, this once-a-year knife skill is not so easy to pull off before an audience. First, fan out the meat slices down the middle, as shown; then add the wings and drumsticks on either end. Garnish with herbs and fruit.

MAKE AHEADS

Best Practice

Prepare as much of this multifaceted meal—particularly the sides and desserts—as possible beforehand so the day itself is more manageable.

1 WEEK BEFORE

TURKEY STOCK: You don't need to wait until you get your bird. You can use turkey wings to make a flavored broth.

SQUASH SEEDS: Roast these (scooped out of any squash you're cooking for another meal) with spices to serve as day-of snacks.

1 TO 3 DAYS BEFORE

PIES: Make pie doughs three days ahead and refrigerate (or better yet, a month in advance and store in the freezer). Bake all pies a day before they will be served to set fruit-pie juices (at room temperature) or custards (in the refrigerator).

MASHED POTATOES: Make them completely, then let cool and refrigerate (covered). To reheat, place the mash in a heatproof bowl set over a saucepan of simmering water; stir until warm.

VEGETABLES: Chop all ingredients for stuffings and sides, then store them in separate labeled airtight containers in the refrigerator.

3 Side-Dish Heroes

Avoid overthinking the sides—it's the turkey that matters most. These simple sauces will elevate practically any steamed or roasted vegetable.

1. BÉCHAMEL: For lovers of creamed spinach or other greens, turn to this easy white sauce (see *marthastewart.com*) made from butter, flour, and milk.

2. BROWN BUTTER: All you need is one ingredient, and heat: Cook butter until the milk solids brown and the flavor becomes nutty. Drizzle over vegetables.

3. VINAIGRETTE: Dress just-roasted vegetables—such as brussels sprouts—with your go-to vinaigrette, and serve warm or at room temperature.

4

WAYS TO

USE
LEFTOVERS

Oh boy, do people love whipping up delicious meals from the remains of the holiday feast. And why not? It takes hours (even days!) to prepare everything, so it's only fitting that you can savor the efforts for days afterward. Breakfast, lunch, and dinner are all here, plus a nourishing broth.

TURKEY BONE BROTH

Place the bones from your turkey (2 to 3 pounds), aromatics (a carrot, celery stalk, quartered onion, bay leaf, and parsley stems), and ½ teaspoon of black peppercorns in a multicooker. Add water to cover; cook on low for 8 hours. (Alternatively, simmer in a Dutch oven, covered, for 6 to 8 hours.) Strain and skim off fat. Let cool; refrigerate in airtight containers up to 1 week, or freeze up to 6 months.

OPEN-FACE SANDWICH

Mix ½ cup mayonnaise, 1 teaspoon grated lemon zest, 1 tablespoon lemon juice, and freshly ground pepper. In another bowl, mix 2 cups diced roasted turkey, ½ cup each diced green apple and celery, ¼ cup celery leaves or parsley, 2 tablespoons lemon juice, 3 tablespoons extra-virgin olive oil, and 2 tablespoons mayo mixture. Spread more mayo on bread; top with turkey salad, sliced cucumbers, and watercress.

CHICKEN À LA CRANBERRY

Season 4 whole chicken legs; brown on both sides in a cast-iron skillet coated with olive oil. Transfer to plate; pour off all but 2 tablespoons fat from pan. Sauté 2 minced shallots. Add 2 tablespoons sherry vinegar; boil 30 seconds. Add 1 cup leftover cranberry sauce and ½ cup chicken broth; simmer until a glaze. Return chicken, skin-side up, to pan; spoon sauce mixture over. Roast at 375°F until thigh reaches 165°F.

POTATOES AND SHIRRED EGGS

Divide 1 cup mashed potatoes between two 6-ounce ramekins. Crack a large egg into each; place in a baking dish. Fill with enough hot water to come 1 inch up sides. Cover with parchment-lined foil. Bake at 375°F until egg whites are set, 20 to 25 minutes. Uncover; let stand 5 minutes. Sprinkle with flaky sea salt and freshly ground pepper. Serve with toast points and chopped fresh chives.

Christmas

A Glittering Tabletop Tree

Decorate a tabletop tree in wintry shades and shapes from nature.

SHIMMERY STRANDS: String pieces of clear and light-pink quartz on jewelry wire; add a loop to each end, and hang from metallic cord.

JEWEL PENDANT: Thread gold cord through the loop on an agate pendant (remove its jump ring first, if necessary), then hang.

MARBLED ORNAMENTS: Remove metal top from a clear glass bulb ornament; add a teaspoon each of two paint colors mixed with marbling medium; swirl; and dry. Or, for extra flash, brush glue on bottom and roll in glitter.

ICY GARLANDS: Use a small crafts saw to cut clear acrylic tubing into 3-inch pieces; string them on gray cord, separated by crystalline chalcedony beads.

Botanical Ornaments

Want to make a lasting impression? Give out handmade ornaments that capture nature with fossil-like charm. To make, roll out paper clay (plain white, or tinted with a few drops of craft paint). Place seasonal greenery (rosemary, spruce, ferns, and dried berries) on top; roll over them to leave imprint. Gently peel away greenery. Punch out rounds with a cookie cutter, poke a hole for hanging with twine, and let dry (pressed with heavy books to keep flat).

Needle Sachets

Scoop up fallen evergreen needles to make fragrant sachets. Stamp muslin bags with snowflake designs; replace the drawstring with red-and-white bakers' twine, and cinch tight. Nestle the sachets into drawers—their scent will last for months.

Tip

To give an ornament a sturdy, secure hanger, thread a 5-inch piece of 28-gauge wire through its loop and twist. Then wrap the other end around the tree branch.

Easy Wreath Upgrade

If your busy holiday schedule doesn't allow for making a wreath from scratch, personalize a plain store-bought one instead. To replicate this example, string two strands of metallic globe lights through an 18-inch juniper wreath, and secure with floral wire. Hang on your front door (or other prominent outside spot) for a welcoming glow.

Miniature Tree Mantel Display

Bottle-brush trees are a longstanding tradition—you can find both new and vintage ones online (the littlest ones here are from a model train set). Arrange a generous grouping of them in a mix of heights and hues along your hearth to transform it into a mini winter wonderland. Tuck in a few flickering votives to add warmth to the snowy scene.

Poinsettia Parade

One of these holiday favorites is good. Many is even better! There are new varieties available of *Euphorbia pulcherrima* (aka poinsettia) in a range of pretty hues—soft pinks (from left, 'Peppermint Ruffles' and 'Princettia Pink'), rich yellow ('Autumn Leaves'), and pale green ('Envy') included. If you'd like a breathy update on the potted-plant tradition, try placing single stems of the cut flowers into mismatched vessels.

4
WAYS TO
MAKE A HOLIDAY COUNTDOWN

Get your family in the spirit of the season by giving an age-old tradition a modern twist. Out are those store-bought calendars with "windows" that open to reveal an image and/or phrase. What's in are DIY numbered displays that are as much festive décor as they are vessels for 8 or 24 surprise gifts.

HANGING ORGANIZER

A 24-pair canvas shoe bag happens to have just the right number of compartments, which are roomy enough to hold wrapped gifts, stuffed animals, and simple (non-digital) games and toys. Consider kitting out a few of the pockets—art supplies in number 6, baking tools in number 9, and so on. For a Hanukkah-appropriate take, trim off a few rows to leave only this holiday's eight nights.

ENVELOPE DISPLAY

Turn a spare wall into an advent gallery by arranging different-size red envelopes in a Christmas tree shape. Use painters' tape to secure them to the wall (without damaging the paint), with their openings facing out and marked with adhesive numbers. Organize them in ascending order or randomly, as here. Fill each one with slim, lightweight presents, such as gift cards, stickers, coloring books and pencils, even cash.

PEGBOARD AND BAGS

Pegboard—this panel is 2 by 4 feet—is the foundation of this pop-up advent calendar. Paint it a festive red and let it dry overnight. Paint numbers on muslin drawstring bags using craft paint, a brush or sponge, and stencils; let them dry overnight as well. Fill each bag with little treats and other loot, and hang them in order on evenly spaced wooden pegs or S hooks. Rest the board on a table or mount on a wall, within easy reach.

MANTEL TREES

The stockings are hung here, so why not put the countdown calendar here too? This lovely landscape works equally well for Hanukkah (shown here) or Christmas—just pick the appropriate number of twinkling trees. To make, cover paper cones in spray adhesive and metallic glitter (or coat with metallic spray paint); attach a paper tag with a number sticker to each one. Hide treats under the cones.

Gift Wrap Upgrade

Give lackluster bulk or recycled paper glints of gold: Spray-paint clean lines (marked with painters' tape) across each sheet, or create a softer effect by going over some bands twice. Using a small brush, you can dab or splatter on acrylic paint (thinned with water for a light touch).

Découpage Party Favors

No one leaves without a gift! For a can't-miss holiday party favor display, create a mosaic of patterned paper-covered boxes. Measure total area of assembled square; cut paper to match. Mark a grid on back of paper, using a lid as a guide. Cut out squares, keeping them in position. Apply Mod Podge adhesive to lids with a paintbrush; press on paper, smoothing any wrinkles. Let dry 24 hours.

Plant Gift Bags

When presenting seasonal plants—amaryllis, rosemary, orchid, paperwhite, mini boxwood—to party hosts and other special someones, ditch the cellophane wrapper. Instead, go for an upcycled gift bag. Spray-paint a brown paper sack (and matching card stock plant tag) in a metallic shade; let dry. Fold down a cuff at the top of the bag for contrast.

Homemade Candles

Using a stack of inexpensive copper bowls (sold at crafts stores and online), you can make handcrafted candles for a season's worth of party hosts, or all of your children's teachers. Tint melted soy wax or leave it natural; add essential oils as desired (about 40 drops oil per cup of wax is a good ratio). Secure wick in bowl, then fill to ¼ inch below rim. Include a plain matchbook, then weave a color-coordinated cord around each set to complete the gift.

Handmade Touches to Photo Cards

To keep your photo cards from feeling generic or getting lost in the pile, add some colorful, personalized details. Print the cards in black-and-white, or order them with a matte finish, to better contrast with your accents. Then add sparkle—a bedecked tree, as here, or a starry sky. Dot on glue, sprinkle with glitter, and tap off excess before sending.

Custom Cocktail Napkins

When the occasion calls for something nicer than paper napkins, try these no-sew fabric ones. Start with lightweight, loose-weave linen cut into 10½-inch squares; fringe the border by pulling out several threads with a pin. Finish with a monogram in one corner, made with a rubber stamp and fabric ink. Go for a contrasting hue, or for a more subtle effect, just a darker shade of the napkin color.

Ribbon Board Card Display

Wondering how to show off all those heartfelt (and artful) greetings from family and friends? Suspend them on an inspiration board. This one has elastic trim that keeps slippery items in place. Begin by covering foam core (or bulletin or corkboard) with fabric, pinning (or stapling) it tightly in back. Cut 10 pieces of trim long enough to wrap around board. Secure evenly spaced horizontal bands first (pin in back); repeat with the verticals, weaving them over and under the rest.

Rickrack Cards

Thanks to its whimsical waves, this trim is tailor-made for shaping into seasonal symbols (featured in December 2002). Glue your rickrack designs to blank cards: Use strips of green for a Christmas tree; add a gold topper and brown stand. Snip white Vs to make a snowflake. For a striped wreath and candy cane, twist together two contrasting strands of equal width; same for the menorah candles, using same-color trim.

Snowflake Cookies Made Easy ›

No, you don't need a fancy iron or other tools to make these splendid pastries. All it takes is good old-fashioned paper-snowflake skills, and a secret shortcut—store-bought wonton wrappers! One inexpensive package has as many as fifty 3½-inch squares, so you (and your kids) can use them to make dozens at a time, and no two will be alike. Fold each square into a triangle, and snip shapes into the edges with kitchen shears. Then unfold them, fry, and dust with confectioners' sugar. These are best the day they're made.

Mint Cookie Toppers

With their iconic swirly design, starlight peppermints will make any cookie (these are chocolate chunk) more celebratory—and more crunchy. Heat the candies in the oven until they are melting, then cover them with parchment and press flat with a baking sheet; place one mint atop each baked treat, adhering with a dab of melted white chocolate.

Pandoro Showstopper

Panettone's loftier, star-shaped cousin, Pandoro (the name means golden bread) is another traditional Christmas dessert that hails from Verona. Should you be the lucky recipient of one of these store-bought specialties, you'll want to give it the spotlight it deserves: Slice the cake horizontally in even intervals (this one is split six ways), then restack and stagger pieces, so their points form an evergreen-tree shape. Top with sugared cranberries, and dust with sifted confectioners' sugar "snow." *Buon Natale!*

Hanukkah

Glass Vase Menorah

If you don't have a cherished heirloom—or are yearning for a holiday update—you can create a modern menorah that keeps the focus on the candles. Simply arrange eight same-size bud vases in a row and place a taller one in the middle. Insert tapers—they'll almost appear to be floating, which seems fitting for the Festival of Lights. For added stability (and fire safety), put candle glue in the bottom of each vase. After the holiday, the vessels will make handy holders for small blooms and greenery.

Handmade Gelt

Why settle for store-bought coins? This traditional treat is so easy to make, and you can personalize your toppings. Melt 2.5 ounces dark chocolate in 10-second increments in the microwave, stirring in between. Divide evenly among 12 greased mini muffin cups. Top with cacao nibs, orange-zest strips, chopped candied ginger, or other garnishes as desired. Refrigerate 30 minutes. Using a small offset spatula, remove the chocolates; blot any excess oil. Wrap in gold or silver candy papers. Refrigerate in an airtight container for up to a week.

Golden-Block Menorah

Transform wooden building blocks and balls into a gilded menorah with hardware-store staples. Cut a ⅜-by-12-inch brass tube into nine pieces with a tube cutter. Stack and arrange wooden pieces as desired to create nine holders; drill holes slightly wider than tube in center of each top piece. Assemble with all-purpose adhesive and a tube piece in each hole; let dry. Spray-paint pieces gold; let dry. Arrange and add candles.

Menorah To Go

When gathering together is not an option, you can still mark the occasion with this special delivery. Head to an office-supply store (or shop online) for the materials, including a "top-open" envelope (one that's long and skinny works best) and washi tape for the menorah. Choose a pattern, like this stripe, for the candles, with a taller center taper; cut bright yellow tape into flame shapes. Then stamp or write "1" through "8" on small gift envelopes (look for color-coordinating ones). Fill each one with a gift, tuck them into the larger envelope, and mail in a padded parcel.

Gift Packages

Give blue-and-white paper goodie bags a new shape by going against their folds. First, place sweets or trinkets in a bag—one for each night—then bring the two corners of its opening together; fold the top over several times. Print tags (see page 282 for template) onto card stock (or just use number stamps and/or handwrite); cut out. Secure to bags with mini clothespins, found at crafts stores.

Star Topper

With store-bought puff pastry in your freezer, no-fuss finales are always within reach—just tuck a buttery pastry shape into ice cream, and dessert is served. Roll out thawed frozen puff pastry ¼ inch thick. Cut out a star (or other holiday figure) with a cookie cutter. Brush with lightly beaten egg; sprinkle with coarse sanding sugar. Bake according to package directions, then let cool.

New Year's Eve

Champagne Toasts

Here are three ways to celebrate auld lang syne with panache.

1. FOR A DRINK-MEETS-DESSERT: Scoop fruit sorbet—raspberry is shown below, but blood orange would work well too—into a wine goblet, then pour prosecco brut (or other dry sparkling wine) to cover. As the sorbet melts, it will infuse the wine with sweetness, flavor, and a festive hue.

2. MAKE A TWO-TONE SIP: Purée 2 cups fresh or thawed frozen cranberries, 1 cup sugar, and 1 cup vodka in a blender until smooth. Strain and chill until cold (about 1 hour), or up to 1 week in an airtight container. Fill a Champagne flute a quarter of the way with purée mixture. To create the ombré effect, tilt flute and gently pour sparkling wine down one side.

3. TWEAK A CLASSIC: Champagne cocktails are usually garnished with a sugar cube soaked in (brown) Angostura bitters. Instead, color sugar cubes with a few drops of a more vibrant liqueur, such as Peychaud's Bitters, crème de violette, or Giffard Pamplemousse. Offer a variety of tinted cubes and let each guest pick a favorite.

Fruit Wreath

Over the course of an evening, ice cubes will only end up diluting a chilled punch—and you have to keep replenishing them. Instead, ring in the New Year with a circle of frozen fruit that keeps the punch cold while imparting brightness and holiday appeal. In a 10-inch Bundt pan, overlap 5 thinly sliced oranges, 2 thinly sliced lemons, 1½ cups whole cranberries, and ¼ cup rosemary sprigs; add 3 cups water and 3 cups cranberry-juice cocktail. Freeze overnight. To unmold wreath, dip pan in a bowl of hot water until edges just start to melt, being careful not to let any water get inside. Invert onto a platter. If not serving immediately, wrap in plastic and freeze up to a month.

Budget Décor

Decorating on a dime is easy when you customize some basic (dollar-store) party supplies. Specifically, embellish round Mylar balloons—mix white, silver, and select colors—with letter, number, and dot stickers to give them a New Year's theme. Think countdown clocks (use extra sticker strips and inside of letters V and O for clock hands and center dot), cheerful messages, and even confetti—no cleanup required! For a makeshift garland, wrap fringed party horns with metallic origami paper (secure with double-sided tape), then thread together with a needle and monofilament; tie a knot in between each horn to keep them in place. Set the scene with more shimmery decorations, such as silver star fans. Post-party, be sure to recycle all the supplies (no balloons escaping into the night!).

Tinsel Toppers

Don't pack away those silvery garlands after Christmas. Repurpose them to make glitzy-in-a-good-way cocktail stirrers. For each one, snip off a short piece of garland, then attach to the end of a bamboo skewer using hot glue. Cut the skewers to fit your glasses as needed—and make extra to prop up in little vases or for revelers to shake (a la pom-poms) at the stroke of midnight.

Oysters on Ice

If an abundant platter of oysters on the half shell is to be your party's pièce de résistance, you'll need a way to keep the mollusks properly chilled—and securely in place. Solution: Fill a (very) large metal serving bowl almost to the top with water and freeze it. Then cover with a bed of crushed ice, arrange evergreen boughs (from your tree or other trimmings) around the perimeter, and lay the just-shucked oysters on top. Serve with plenty of lemon wedges as well as cocktail sauce, mignonette, and horseradish.

Tip Oysters should be refrigerated until shucking (up to 2 days): Nestle them deep-side down on a bed of ice, cover with a damp cloth, and check often—do not allow them to sit in water.

Shucking Oysters

Shucking takes practice, but after your first dozen you'll be doing it like a pro. This technique is from Norm Bloom, owner of Copps Island Oysters in Norwalk, Connecticut. (Always protect your hand with a towel—those shells are sharp.)

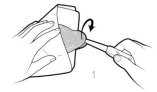

1. FIND THE HINGE: Insert the tip of a shucking knife into the muscle that holds the shells together at the bottom tip. Turn it like a key until it pops open.

2. SLICE IT OPEN: Scrape the knife along the top to slice the muscle. (Be careful not to damage the meat.) Clean any sand or grit from the bottom shell.

3. RELEASE THE OYSTER: Glide the knife underneath the meat to separate it from the adductor muscle, without spilling the oyster liquor (aka the liquid inside). Serve on ice.

Templates

Stain Chart

See "Stain Chart," page 62. The solutions below are for washable items only.
See * opposite for how to make the diluted dishwashing-soap solution.

GREASE (butter, oil, mayonnaise)	Treat area with a dry solvent (such as mineral spirits or acetone) in a well-ventilated room. Using an eyedropper, rinse with isopropyl alcohol; dry well. Spray diluted dishwashing-soap solution on any remaining residue, and soak the item in an enzyme detergent before washing.
PROTEIN (blood, egg)	Spray diluted dishwashing-soap solution on stain, and let it sit; rinse in tepid water. If stain remains, treat area with an enzyme detergent, and wash according to label instructions.
FRUIT OR VEGETABLE (juice, jam)	Spray diluted dishwashing-soap solution on the stain to remove sugars. Using an eyedropper, flush the area with white vinegar and then hydrogen peroxide to remove any remaining color. Follow up with an enzyme detergent to remove residue before washing.
GRASS	Treat area with a dry solvent in a well-ventilated room. Press with cheesecloth; tamp with a soft-bristled brush. Repeat to remove as much pigment as possible. Flush area with isopropyl alcohol, tamp, and let dry. Follow up with an enzyme detergent to remove residue before washing.
RED WINE	Spray diluted dishwashing-soap solution on stain; tamp with a soft-bristled brush. Flush with water, apply white vinegar, and tamp; let stand several minutes; flush again. If stain remains, apply hydrogen peroxide, and let stand. If stain persists, apply 1 or 2 drops of ammonia to wet area. Flush with water. Treat with an enzyme detergent; wash. If stain is still there, apply a powdered nonchlorinated color-safe bleach, such as sodium percarbonate; rewash.
WHITE WINE	Flush the stain with cold water, and spray with diluted dishwashing-soap solution. Treat area with an enzyme detergent, and then wash.
COFFEE OR TEA	Using an eyedropper, flush area with lemon juice or white vinegar to remove stain; then treat with stronger bleach, if necessary. To help remove sugar or milk, spray area with diluted dishwashing-soap solution, then wash with an enzyme detergent.
CHOCOLATE	Gently scrape off excess chocolate; spray area with diluted dishwashing-soap solution. Follow up with an enzyme detergent to remove residue before washing.
LIPSTICK	Use a dull-edged knife to remove excess lipstick. Using an eyedropper, apply a dry solvent (such as mineral spirits or acetone) in a well-ventilated room; tamp with a soft-bristled brush. Flush area with isopropyl alcohol, and tamp. Repeat until all stain is removed, and let dry. Spray with diluted dishwashing-soap solution. Treat with an enzyme detergent, and wash.

WAX OR GUM	Use ice to freeze wax or gum, or place item in the freezer; scrape or crack off as much as you can, then remove residue with an oil solvent or mineral spirits. Rinse with isopropyl alcohol; let dry. Treat with an enzyme detergent; wash.
MUSTARD	Using an eyedropper, flush stain with vinegar; then wash with diluted dishwashing-soap solution.
SAUCES (tomato, ketchup, barbecue)	Scrape off sauce; spray area with diluted dishwashing-soap solution. Soak in tepid water. If color remains, apply white vinegar with an eyedropper. Treat with an enzyme detergent; wash. If color persists, apply several drops of hydrogen peroxide; let sit. Rinse; treat again with enzyme detergent, and wash.
SOY SAUCE	Spray with diluted dishwashing-soap solution; tamp with a soft-bristled brush. Flush with water, apply white vinegar, and tamp; let stand several minutes, and flush again. If stain remains, apply hydrogen peroxide, and let stand. If stain persists, apply 1 or 2 drops of ammonia to wet area. Flush with water. Treat with an enzyme detergent; wash. If stain is still there, apply a powdered nonchlorinated color-safe bleach, such as sodium percarbonate; rewash.
VINAIGRETTE	First, treat stain as a grease stain (see Grease, left). Then flush with white vinegar to remove any remaining spot. Follow up with an enzyme detergent to remove residue before washing.
FELT-TIP INK	First, determine whether the ink is oil-based or water-based by building a "dam" around the stain with mineral oil or petroleum jelly; work within the confines of the dam. Test the ink with a cotton swab saturated with water and another one saturated with isopropyl alcohol. If isopropyl alcohol pulls more pigment out of the stain, follow the steps for ballpoint ink stains below. If water is more effective, spray the stain with diluted dishwashing-soap solution, then flush with cold water. Alternately, to remove permanent marker, apply Amodex Ink & Stain Remover to the stained area. For fabrics, gently rub with a brush, then rinse or launder.
BALLPOINT INK	Build a "dam" around the stain with mineral oil or petroleum jelly. Always work within the confines of the dam. Treat area with isopropyl alcohol using an eyedropper. Remove any remaining pigment with a dry solvent in a well-ventilated room; let dry. Rinse with diluted dishwashing-soap solution, then wash with an enzyme detergent in warm water.
MUD	If stain is a combination of mud and grass, treat grass stain first (see Grass, left). Shake or scrape off residue; pretreat stain with diluted dishwashing-soap solution, and soak. Then treat with an enzyme detergent; wash.

The diluted-soap solution called for above is made with 1 tablespoon of fragrance- and dye-free liquid soap (containing sodium laurel sulfate, or sodium laureth sulfate) and 9.5 ounces of water. Pour it into a tiny spray bottle. Do not use the enzyme detergent, called for above, on protein fibers, such as silk, wool, cashmere, or angora. Always wash fabric after using a dry solvent (such as mineral spirits or acetone), and do not use acetone on acetate. Amodex is a nontoxic cream effective at removing everyday stains including ink, food stains, grease/oil, wine, blood, grass, and more from most fabrics.

Heart-and-Arrow Pens

See "Heart-and-Arrow Pens," page 218. Photocopy template at desired size onto 8½-by-11-inch paper; cut out.

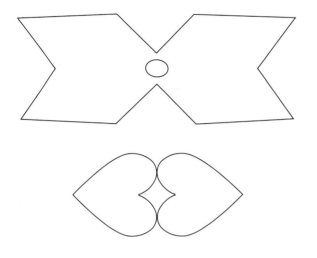

Heart Photo

See "Heart Photo," page 229. Photocopy template at desired size onto 8½-by-11-inch paper; cut out.

Trivia Quiz Booklet

See "Trivia Quiz Booklet," page 247. Photocopy artwork (see right) at desired size, and trim along border. Using a craft knife, cut along the solid line at the center of the page.

1. Start with the paper held horizontally. Fold in half lengthwise, and reopen. Fold in half widthwise, and reopen.

2. Fold again into quarters widthwise, starting from the outside and folding toward the center. Reopen.

3. Fold in half widthwise, then push ends together till page marked "Question 5" touches page marked "Question 11."

4. Using the cover art as a guide, close to form booklet. Numbers will be in consecutive order if folded correctly.

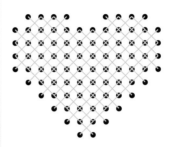

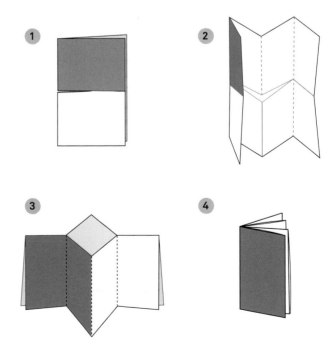

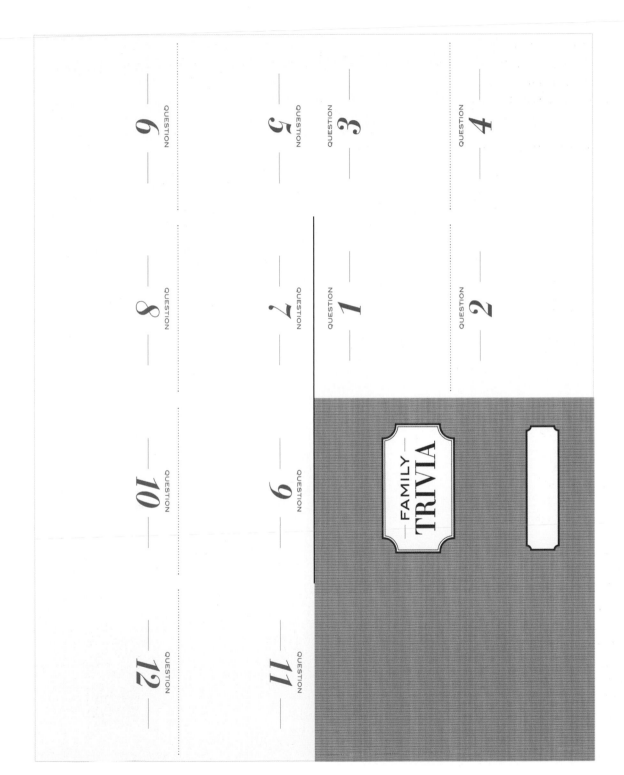

QUESTION 4

QUESTION 3

QUESTION 2

QUESTION 1

QUESTION 5

QUESTION 6

QUESTION 7

QUESTION 8

FAMILY TRIVIA

QUESTION 9

QUESTION 10

QUESTION 11

QUESTION 12

Pressed-Leaf Animals

See "Pressed-Leaf Animals," page 249. Photocopy template at desired size onto 8½-by-11-inch paper; cut out.

Leaf Trivets

See "Leaf Trivets," page 252. Photocopy the leaf design at desired size, then trace onto a square piece of corkboard (available at most office-supply stores) with permanent marker. Place corkboard on a cutting mat, and cut along the outline with a craft knife. Turn over to display.

Gift Package Tags

See "Gift Packages," page 271. Photocopy tags at desired size onto card stock and cut out.

Index

Credits

Photo Credits

Front cover: Fadil Berisha

Lucas Allen: 24 (right); Sang An: 162 (left), 265 (bottom); Gieves Anderson: 212, 222 (right), 225 (bottom), 226 (right); Peter Ardito: 65 (top left), 105 (left), 116 (top left), 124, 148 (right), 266 (right); Burcu Avsar: 10, 46 (left), 68 (left), 86 (right), 92 (bottom and top right), 98, 102 (top), 126 (right, pairings), 129, 197 (top right), 210 (left), 218 (bottom), 229 (left), 271 (top); James Baigrie: 94 (top right); Christopher Baker: 5 (bottom right), 223 (top right); Roland Bello: 243 (right); Sidney Bensimon: 5 (bottom left), 49 (left), 81 (top right), 154 (left), 205 (bottom); Justin Bernhaut: 21 (right), 222 (left); Petra Bindel: 2, 196; Monica Buck: 55 (right); Jennifer Causey: 57, 97 (left), 100 (top left), 107 (left), 210 (right), 234 (bottom right); Chelsea Cavanaugh: 1, 5 (top middle), 29, 34, 41, 46 (right), 59 (left), 65 (bottom), 92 (top left), 95, 149 (bottom right), 158 (top right), 185, 189, 217, 224 (left), 232 (left), 234 (top); 238 (top right), 248 (left), 200–201; Ted Cavanaugh: 237; Joseph De Leo: 206; Pippa Drummond: 24 (left), 104, 181; Aaron Dyer: 5 (top right), 17 (bottom), 25, 28, 30 (left), 40 (top right), 42 (left), 43 (right), 45, 47 (right), 49 (middle), 65 (top left), 68 (right), 73 (right), 77 (right), 80 (right), 83, 88 (bottom left), 90 (top), 96 (left), 100 (top right), 105 (right), 108, 114, 120 (left), 153 (bottom), 174 (right), 178 (bottom), 183 (top), 183 (bottom right), 188 (right), 191, 193 (4), 194 (left), 197 (left), 204, 216, 218 (top left), 220 (top right), 224 (right), 225 (top left, egg photographs), 226 (left), 228 (left), 230 (right), 231 (left), 233 (left, top right, bottom right), 235 (left, top right), 247 (left), 249 (left), 268 (bottom), 270, 272, 273; Diane Fields: 182, 235 (bottom right); Johnny Fogg: 23, 40 (top left), 107 (right), 110 (top right), 164 (right), 178 (top), 198 (left), 229 (right), 234 (bottom left); Kristen Francis: 17 (top), 26, 36, 37, 39 (bottom), 78, 81 (top left), 86 (left), 87, 106 (right), 148 (left), 227, 246, 254 (left), 255 (left), 257 (right), 263 (top left), 264 (top and bottom), 266 (left), 269, 272 (left); Nicole Franzen: 53 (top), 61, 170; Dana Gallagher: 110 (left), 171; Bryan Gardner: 12, 21 (left), 39 (top), 52 (right), 101 (bottom left), 119 (top right), 127 (bottom), 127 (top right), 128 (left), 130 (right), 134 (top right), 139, 144, 146 (right), 150, 154 (right), 155, 158 (top left), 159 (bottom right), 163, 180 (right), 186 (left), 187 (left), 188 (top left), 190 (right), 202 (top), 211 (left), 220 (bottom), 244 (right), 254 (right), 257 (bottom); Gentl and Hyers: 88 (right); Getty: 36 (four-part portrait: top left image, bottom left image, bottom right image), 71 (right); Getty/Ralf Turander: 50, 55 (left); Hans Gissinger: 190 (left); John Gruen: 18 (left), 122 (left); Louise Hagger: 145, 120–121 (center); Raymond Hom: 5 (bottom middle), 18 (left), 54, 160, 162 (right), 173 (bottom), 180 (left), 193 (#1–3), 195 (left), 199, 202 (bottom), 209 (bottom), 221, 274 (left); Lisa Hubbard: 30 (right), 121 (right); Ingalls Photography: 77 (left), 157 (left); Inside/Closet: 20 (right); Stephen Kent Johnson: 8, 14, 16, 22 (left), 48; Addie Juell: 19, 20 (left), 47 (left), 236 (right), 238 (bottom right), 239, 240, 241 (left), 260 (right); John Kernick: 157 (right); Yunhee Kim: 33, 43 (left), 67 (right), 109 (top left), 134 (bottom right), 203, 205 (top), 211 (right); Mike Krautter: 152; Stephen Lewis: 38; Vanessa Lewis: 208; Ryan Liebe: 32, 44, 49 (right), 66 (right), 67 (left), 93, 125 (right), 138 (left), 244 (left), 245, 251 (left), 258 (top, bottom), 259, 261 (left), 268 (top); Pernille Loof: 59 (right), 106 (left), 176–177, 214 (bottom), 218 (top right), 256, 261 (right), 263 (top right), 267; Thomas Loof: 275; Ellen McDermott: 159 (left); Charles Masters: 53 (bottom); Kate Mathis: 26, 40 (bottom), 42 (right), 63 (bottom), 66 (left), 71 (left), 82 (bottom), 83 (top), 91, 100 (bottom), 103, 110 (bottom right), 111, 206 (bottom), 214 (top right), 215, 231 (bottom right), 247 (right), 262 (left), 265 (top); Maura McEvoy: 188 (bottom left); David Meredith: 94 (bottom); James Merrell: 263 (right); Ellie Miller: 238 (left); Johnny Miller: 6, 31, 56 (left), 64, 70 (left), 88 (top left), 89 (top right), 89 (bottom), 96 (right), 97 (right), 101 (bottom right), 140, 159 (top right), 192 (top right), 192 (bottom), 198 (right), 207, 223 (top left), 223 (bottom), 271 (bottom); The Morrisons: 232 (right), 236 (left), 241 (right); Michael Mundy: 90 (bottom); Ngoc Minh Ngo: 15, 76; Marcus Nilsson: 90 (bottom), 125 (top), 126 (left), 146 (left), 149 (left, burrito photographs), 149 (top right), 156, 164 (left), 168, 169, 183 (bottom left), 252 (right), 253; Helen Norman: 80 (left); Kana Okada: 109 (right), 214 (top left), 220 (top left); Victoria Pearson: 72; Eric Piasecki: 60 (top right); Con Poulos: 123, 153 (top), 166, 167; David Prince: 62 (right), 184 (right), 194 (right); Linda Pugliese: 118; Andrew Purcell: 231 (top); Sharon Radisch: 187 (right); Armando Rafael: 209 (top); Sammy Ruppert: 36 (four-part portrait, top right image) Annie Schlechter: 84 (right), 102 (bottom); Victor Schrager: 75; Kate Sears: 175; Chris Simpson: 131; Alpha Smoot: 35 (left), 174 (left), 248 (right), 249 (right), 250; Seth Smoot: 22 (right), 69, 74 (top), 84 (left), 94 (top right), 116 (right), 165 (left), 228 (right), 252 (left), 260 (right); Martha Stewart: 60 (top left); Tim Street-Porter/OTTO: 58; Christopher Testani: 127 (top left), 141, 142 (left), 142 (right), 143 (left), 143 (right), 147, 184, 251 (right); Martyn Thompson: 52 (left), 242–243; Petrina Tinslay: 136 (top); Trevor Tondro/OTTO: 13, 115 (right); Jonny Valient: 89 (top left); Mikkel Vang: 172, 173 (top); Justin Walker: 132–133, 135, 255 (left); Lennart Weibull: 5 (top left), 11, 35 (right), 85, 99, 117, 219, 230 (left); Anna Williams: 112, 119 (bottom), 151, 179; Dasha Wright: 81 (bottom); Romulo Yanes: 122 (right), 137, 186 (right), 192 (top left)

Back cover, clockwise from top left: Seth Smoot, Burcu Avsar, Chelsea Cavanaugh, Alpha Smoot, Johnny Fogg, Gieves Anderson

All illustrations by Kate Francis / Brown Bird Design

Additional Credits

This book was produced by

MELCHER
MEDIA

124 West 13th Street • New York, NY 10011 • melcher.com

FOUNDER, CEO: Charles Melcher
VP, COO: Bonnie Eldon
EDITORIAL DIRECTOR: Lauren Nathan
PRODUCTION DIRECTOR: Susan Lynch
SENIOR EDITOR: Megan Worman

CONTRIBUTING EDITOR: Evelyn Battaglia
ART DIRECTOR: Laura Palese
DESIGNER/EDITOR: Renée Bollier

Acknowledgments

First and foremost, Melcher Media would like to thank the great Martha Stewart and her team, especially our unflappable teammate and leader, Susanne Ruppert; Kevin Sharkey and the team at Marquee Brands for their support; and Kim Dumer and Ryan Mesina for their exhaustive help with photo rights. We're also grateful to Laura Wallis, as well as to our wonderful partners at Houghton Mifflin Harcourt, specifically Deb Brody, Karen Murgolo, Stephanie Fletcher, and Tai Blanche. Finally, we'd like to thank all of our other colleagues who contributed in various ways, including Amélie Cherlin, Cheryl Della Pietra, Shannon Fanuko, Luke Gernert, Zoe Margolis, Carolyn Merriman, Vanina Morrison, Elizabeth Parson, Nola Romano, and Christopher Steighner.